English Grammar for Students of Italian

The Study Guide
for Those Learning Italian

Third edition

Sergio Adorni
University of Windsor

Karen Primorac
University of Michigan

The Olivia and Hill Press®

THE O&H STUDY GUIDES
Jacqueline Morton, editor

English Grammar for Students of French
English Grammar for Students of Spanish
English Grammar for Students of German
English Grammar for Students of Italian
English Grammar for Students of Latin
English Grammar for Students of Russian
English Grammar for Students of Japanese
English Grammar for Students of Arabic
English Grammar for Students of Chinese
Gramática española para estudiantes de inglés

Printed in the U.S.A.

ISBN: 978-0-934034-40-1

Library of Congress Control Number: 2011921529

CONTENTS

CONTENTS

TO THE STUDENT

English Grammar for Students of Italian explains the grammatical terms and concepts that you will encounter in your Italian textbook and relates them to English grammar. With straightforward explanations and numerous examples, this handbook offers a bridge between English and Italian, indicating similarities and differences. Once you have understood the terms and concepts in your own language, it will be easier for you to understand your textbook.

Since *English Grammar for Students of Italian* can be keyed to any elementary textbook, many instructors assign a specific section as preparation for the study of a given grammatical topic in your Italian textbook. If you use this manual on your own, you can consult the table of contents and index to locate the topic you are about to study. Read the relevant pages carefully, making sure that you understand the explanations and the examples. Do the Reviews provided online and compare your answers with the Answer Key (www.oliviahill.com).

STUDY GUIDE

Before doing an assignment — Read the sections in *English Grammar for Students of Italian* that cover the topics you are going to study and the explanations in your textbook .

Homework — Take notes as you study your textbook. Highlighting is not sufficient. The more often you write down and use vocabulary and rules, the easier it will be for you to remember them. Complete exercises and activities over several short periods of time rather than in one long session.

Written exercises — As you write Italian words or sentences, say them out loud. Each time you write, read, say, or listen to a word, it reinforces it in your memory.

In class — Take notes. You will know what the teacher considers important and it will reinforce what you are studying.

Objective — You have learned something successfully once you are able to take a blank sheet of paper and write a short sentence in Italian using the correct form of the Italian words without reference to a textbook or dictionary. The study tips below will help you with this learning process.

1

10

20

30

TIPS FOR LEARNING VOCABULARY

One aspect of language learning is remembering a number of foreign words.

To learn vocabulary — Flashcards are a good, handy tool for learning new words and their meaning. You can carry flashcards with you, group them as you wish, and add information as you advance. Creating your own flashcards is an important first step in learning vocabulary.

1. Write the Italian word or expression on one side of an index card and its English equivalent on the other side.

2. On the Italian side of the card add a short sentence using the word or expression. It will be easier for you to recall a word in context. To make sure that your sentence is grammatically accurate, copy an example from your textbook. For review purposes, write down the chapter and page number of your textbook where the word is introduced.

3. On the Italian side include any irregularities and whatever information is relevant to the word in question.

How to use the cards — Regardless of the side of the card you're working on, always say the Italian word out loud.

1. Look at the Italian side first. Going from Italian to English is easier than going from English to Italian because it only requires your recognizing the Italian word. Read the Italian word(s) out loud, giving the English equivalent; then, check your answer on the English side.

2. When you go easily from Italian to English, turn the cards to the English side. Going from English to Italian is harder than going from Italian to English because you have to pull the word and its spelling out of your memory. Say the Italian equivalent out loud as you write it down on a separate sheet of paper; then check the spelling with the card. Some students prefer closing their eyes and visualizing the Italian word and its spelling.

3. As you progress, put aside the cards you know and concentrate on the ones you still don't know.

How to remember words — Below are suggestions to help you associate an Italian word with an English word with a similar meaning. This is the first step and it will put the Italian word in your short-term memory. Use and practice, the next step, will put the words in your long-term memory.

1. There are many words, called **COGNATES**, that have the same meaning and approximately the same spelling in English as in Italian. These words are easy to recognize in Italian, but you will have to concentrate on the differences in spelling and pronunciation.

important	importante
problem	problema
visit	visitare

2. Try to associate the Italian word with an English word that has a related meaning.

la luna	*the moon*	lunar
preoccupato	*worried*	preoccupation
l'ascensore	*the elevator*	ascend

3. If the Italian word has no similarities to English, rely on any association, or "hook," that is meaningful to you. Here are some suggestions:

   - Group words by topics or personal associations – You can group words according to topics such as food, clothing, activities you do for fun, sports, school, home, or things you carry in your backpack, etc.
   - Associate the word with an image – If you have trouble remembering a particular word, you might want to create a "bizarre image" in your mind using English words with similar sounds with which to associate it.

     caro = *expensive*
     You're giving me an *expensive* **car** 'Oh, boy!'
     con = *with*
     "He is a **con** man *with* charm."

4. To reinforce the Italian word and its spelling, use it in a short sentence.

TIPS FOR LEARNING WORD FORMS

Another aspect of language learning is remembering the various forms a word can take; for example, another form of *book* is *books* and *do* can take the form of *does* and *did*. As a general rule, the first part of the word indicates its meaning and the second part indicates its form. (See also "Memorizing conjugations," p. 40.)

In bocca al lupo!

Sergio Adorni
Karen Primorac

WHAT'S IN A WORD?

When learning a foreign language, in this case Italian, you must look at every word in three ways: meaning, class, and use.

1. MEANING — You learn new vocabulary in Italian by associating each new word with its English equivalent.

> The English word *book* has the same meaning as Italian **libro**.

Sometimes knowing one Italian word will help you learn other words derived from it.

> Knowing that **latte** means *milk* should help you understand that **lattaio** means *milkman,* **latteria** means *dairy,* and **latticino** means *dairy product.*

Often, however, either there is no similarity between words in English and Italian, or one Italian word is not derived from another. In this case, you must learn each word as a separate vocabulary item.

> Knowing that *man* is **uomo** will not help you learn that *woman* is **donna**.

In addition, there are times when words in combination will take on a special meaning. For instance, when we say "They threw the book at him" we are not really talking about throwing books, but about someone being severely punished. Such an expression, whose meaning as a whole ("to throw the book") is different from the combined meaning of the individual words ("to throw" and "book"), is called an IDIOM.

It is important that you learn to recognize English idioms so that you do not translate them word-for-word into Italian.

> "To have a good time" is not **avere** *to have* + **un buon tempo** *a good time,* but **divertirsi**.

Similarly, you will have to learn to recognize Italian idioms so as not to translate them word-for-word.

> **Fare** means *to make;* **coda** means *tail.* However **fare la coda** means "to line up."

2. CLASS — English and Italian words are grouped in categories called PARTS OF SPEECH. We shall consider eight different parts of speech:

noun	verb
pronoun	adverb
adjective	preposition
article	conjunction

Each part of speech follows its own rules. You must learn to identify the part of speech to which an English word belongs in order to choose the correct Italian equivalent and to use it correctly in a sentence.

In your dictionary, the part of speech is always given in italics right after the word entry. For instance, if you look up "student," you will find "student, *n.*" (noun); if you look up "beautiful," you will find "beautiful, *adj.*" (adjective).

Some words, however, may be used in a variety of ways and, therefore, may belong to more than one part of speech.

Look at the word *that* in the following sentences:

That girl is my sister.	ADJECTIVE
That is not true.	PRONOUN
He was *that* smart.	ADVERB
He said *that* he was busy.	CONJUNCTION

The English word is the same in all four sentences, but in Italian four different words will be used because each *that* belongs to a different part of speech.

3. **USE** — In addition to its classification as to its part of speech, each word has a special **FUNCTION** or use within a sentence. Determining the function of a word will help you to choose the correct Italian form and to know what rules to apply.

Look at the word *him* in the following sentences:

I don't know *him*.	DIRECT OBJECT
Have you told *him?*	INDIRECT OBJECT
Are you going with *him?*	OBJECT OF PREPOSITION

The English word is the same in all three sentences, but in Italian three different words will be used because each *him* has a different function.

CAREFUL — As a student of Italian you must learn to recognize both the part of speech and the function of each word within a sentence. This is important because in Italian, unlike English, the form of most words is determined by their relationship to other words in the sentence.

Compare the following sentences in English and Italian.

The small red **shoes are** *under the small white box.*

Le piccole **scarpe** rosse sono sotto la piccola **scatola** bianca.

IN ENGLISH

The only word that determines the form of another word in the sentence is *shoes,* which requires *are.* (If the word were *shoe,* we would have to use *is.)*

IN ITALIAN

The word for *shoes,* **scarpe,** determines not only the word for *are,* **sono,** but also the form of the words for *the,* **le,** *little,* **piccole,** and *red,* **rosse.** The word for *box,* **scatola,** affects the words for *the,* **la,** *small,* **piccola,** and *white,* **bianca.** The only word which is not affected is the word for *under,* **sotto.**

Since parts of speech and function are usually determined in the same way in English and Italian, this handbook will show you how to identify them in English. You will then learn to compare English and Italian constructions. This will give you a better understanding of the grammar explanations in your Italian textbook.

WHAT IS A NOUN?

A **NOUN** is a word that can be the name of a person, animal, place, thing, event, or idea.

- a person   teacher, boy, Laura, Mancini, friend
- an animal   cat, duck, Fido, Bambi, horse
- a place   city, state, library, Rome, Europe
- a thing   book, house, wine, Sunday, Ferrari
- an event   birth, marriage, Thanksgiving, skiing
  or activity
- an idea   truth, poverty, peace, fear, beauty,
  or concept   love, happiness, democracy

As you can see, a noun is not only a word that names something that is tangible (i.e., something you can see, smell, taste, or touch), such as *Mario, cat, wine* or *Ferrari*, it can also be the name of something that is abstract (i.e., that you cannot touch), such as *truth, peace, democracy,* or *humor*.

A noun that is the name of a specific person, thing, or place *(Mario, Ferrari, Rome)* is called a **PROPER NOUN**. Proper nouns always begin with a capital letter. A noun that does not state the name of specific person, place, or thing, etc. is called a **COMMON NOUN** *(man, car, city)*. Common nouns only begin with a capital letter when they are the first word of a sentence or question.

Teresa is my friend.
proper   common
noun   noun

IN ENGLISH

To help you learn to recognize nouns, look at the paragraph below where the nouns are in *italics*.

Italy produces many agricultural, industrial and artistic *items* which are in *demand* throughout the *world*. The *cultivation* of the *grape* and the *olive* is of great *importance* to the Italian *economy* and many *countries* import fine Italian *wines* and *olive*[1] oil. Among the many industrial *exports* are *automobiles,* sewing *machines* and electrical *appliances*. *Italy* is also famous for its *handicrafts;* among them *leather*[1] goods from *Florence,* glassware from *Venice, coral*[1] jewelry from *Naples,* and *ceramics*

[1] Examples of nouns used as adjectives, see p. 96.

from *Faenza*. The *achievements* of Italian *artists* and *musicians* have been recognized for *centuries* and the *popularity* of Italian *fashion,* industrial *design* and *movies* extends far beyond the *borders* of the *country.*

IN ITALIAN

Nouns are identified the same way as they are in English.

TERMS USED TO TALK ABOUT NOUNS

Gender — In Italian, a noun has a gender; that is, it can be classified according to whether it is masculine or feminine (see *What is Meant by Gender?*, p. 9).

Number — A noun has number; that is, it can be identified as being singular or plural (see *What is Meant by Number?*, p. 13).

Function — A noun can have a variety of functions in a sentence; that is, it can be the subject of the sentence (see *What is a Subject?*, p. 28), or an object (see *What is an Object?*, p. 117).

WHAT IS MEANT BY GENDER?

GENDER in the grammatical sense means that a word can be classified as masculine, feminine, or neuter.

Did Gino give Anna the book? Yes, *he* gave *it* to *her*.
masc. neuter fem.

Grammatical gender is not very important in English. However, it is at the very heart of the Italian language where the gender of a word is often reflected not only in the way the word itself is spelled and pronounced, but also in the way all the words connected to it are spelled and pronounced.

More parts of speech indicate gender in Italian than in English.

ENGLISH	ITALIAN
pronouns	nouns
possessive adjectives	articles
	pronouns
	adjectives

Since each part of speech follows its own rules to indicate gender, you will find gender discussed in the sections dealing with articles and with the various types of pronouns and adjectives. In this section we shall look at the gender of nouns only.

IN ENGLISH

Nouns themselves do not have gender, but sometimes their meaning indicates a gender based on the biological sex of the person or animal the noun represents. For example, when we replace a proper or common noun that refers to one man or woman, we use *he* for males and *she* for females.

- nouns referring to males indicate the MASCULINE gender

  Mario came home; *he* was tired; the dog was glad to see *him*.
  noun (male)   masculine   masculine

- nouns referring to females indicate the FEMININE gender

  Tina came home; *she* was tired; the dog was glad to see *her*.
  noun (female)   feminine   feminine

All the proper or common nouns that do not have a biological gender are considered **NEUTER** and are replaced by *it* when they refer to one thing, place, or idea.

> The *city* of Siena is lovely. I enjoyed visiting *it.*
> 　　　noun　　　　　　　　　　　　　　neuter

There are a few well-known exceptions, such as *ship,* which is referred to as *she.* It is custom, not logic, that decides.

> The USS Nimitz is among the biggest warships in the world. *She* is the lead ship of *her* class.

IN ITALIAN

All nouns — common nouns and proper nouns — have a gender; they are masculine or feminine. Do not confuse these grammatical terms with the biological terms "male" and "female." Only a few Italian nouns have a grammatical gender tied to biological sex; most nouns have a gender that must be memorized.

The gender of nouns based on **BIOLOGICAL GENDER** is easy to determine. These are nouns whose meaning is always tied to one or the other of the biological sexes, male or female.

MALES	MASCULINE	FEMALES	FEMININE
Paul	Paolo	*Mary*	Maria
little boy	bambino	*little girl*	bambina
brother	fratello	*sister*	sorella
grandfather	nonno	*grandmother*	nonna

The gender of most Italian nouns, common and proper, cannot easily be explained or figured out. These nouns have a **GRAMMATICAL GENDER** that is unrelated to biological gender. Here are some examples of English nouns classified under the gender of their Italian equivalent.

	MASCULINE		FEMININE
book	libro	*library*	biblioteca
country	paese	*nation*	nazione
vice	vizio	*virtue*	virtù
Canada	Canada	*Italy*	Italia
Monday	lunedì	*Sunday*	domenica

Textbooks and dictionaries usually indicate the gender of a noun with an *m.* for masculine or an *f.* for feminine. When learning vocabulary you should memorize the noun together with its article since the article usually indicates gender (see *What is an Article?*, p. 15).

CAREFUL — Do not rely on biological gender to indicate the grammatical gender of Italian nouns that can refer to either a male or a female. For instance, the grammatical gender of the noun **la persona** *person* is always feminine, regardless of whether it refers to a man or a woman and the grammatical gender of **il bebè** *baby* is always masculine, even though the baby being referred to could be a boy or a girl.

Italian endings indicating gender

Gender, whether biological or grammatical, can sometimes be determined by the ending of a noun.

- nouns ending in a consonant → always masculine

il bar	*bar*
lo sport	*sport*
il film	*film*
il weekend	*week*

- nouns ending in -o → usually masculine

il libro	*book*
il giorno	*day*
il gatto	*cat*
il maestro	*teacher*

- nouns ending in -a → usually feminine

la carta	*paper*
la rosa	*rose*
la casa	*house*
la maestra	*teacher*

- nouns ending in -i → usually feminine

l'analisi	*analysis*
la tesi	*thesis*
l'enfasi	*emphasis*

- nouns ending in -e → can be masculine or feminine

l'attore *m.*	*actor*
l'attrice *f.*	*actress*
il motore *m.*	*motor*
la lezione *f.*	*lesson*

As you can see from the above examples, unless we are referring to a masculine or feminine being, the gender of a noun in -e is not easily identifiable. There are, however, certain -e endings which are more predictable.

- nouns ending in **-ie, -trice, -zione,** or **-dine** → always feminine

la ser**ie**	*series*
la mo**trice**	*train engine*
la le**zione**	*lesson*
la solitu**dine**	*solitude*

There are a few exceptions to the above rules, for instance, **la mano** *the hand* is a feminine noun even though it ends in **-o; il problema** *the problem* is a masculine noun even though it ends in **-a.** Your textbook and instructor will point out additional exceptions.

WHAT IS MEANT BY NUMBER?

NUMBER in the grammatical sense is the designation of a [1]
word as singular or plural. When a word refers to one person
or thing, it is said to be SINGULAR; when it refers to more than
one, it is called PLURAL.

More parts of speech have number in Italian than in English.

ENGLISH	ITALIAN
nouns	nouns
verbs	verbs
pronouns	pronouns
demonstrative adjectives	adjectives
	articles [10]

Since each part of speech follows its own rules to indicate
number, you will find number discussed in the sections
dealing with verbs, pronouns, adjectives, and articles. In this
section we will only look at the number of nouns.

IN ENGLISH

We indicate the plural of nouns in several ways:

- most commonly by adding an "-s" or "-es" to a singular
  noun

book	book*s*	[20]
kiss	kiss*es*	

- sometimes by making a spelling change

man	m*e*n
leaf	lea*ves*
child	child*ren*

Some nouns, called COLLECTIVE NOUNS, refer to a group of
persons or things, but they are considered singular.

A soccer *team has* eleven players.
The *family is* well.
The *crowd was* quiet. [30]

IN ITALIAN

As in English, the plural of a word is usually spelled and
pronounced differently from its singular form.

Singular nouns are made plural according to three basic rules.

▪ nouns ending in -o or -e change to -i

libro	libri	*book*	*books*
ragazzo	ragazzi	*boy*	*boys*
giornale	giornali	*newspaper*	*newspapers*
lezione	lezioni	*lesson*	*lessons*

▪ nouns ending in -a change to -e

casa	case	*house*	*houses*
ragazza	ragazze	*girl*	*girls*

▪ nouns ending in a vowel with a written accent, an -i, or a consonant do not change

città	città	*city*	*cities*
virtù	virtù	*virtue*	*virtues*
analisi	analisi	*analysis*	*analyses*
tesi	tesi	*thesis*	*theses*
bar	bar	*bar*	*bars*
film	film	*film*	*films*

Your textbook will point out exceptions to these basic rules.

As in English, collective nouns refer to a group of persons or things, and are considered singular.

La **squadra** di calcio ha undici giocatori.
*The soccer **team** has eleven players.*

La **famiglia** sta bene.
*The **family** is well.*

La **folla** era calma.
*The **crowd** was quiet.*

CAREFUL — A few nouns change gender when they become plural, for example: **l'uovo** (m.) → **le uova** (f.) *egg, eggs;* **il braccio** (m.) → **le braccia** (f.) *arm, arms.*

CHAPTER

5

WHAT IS AN ARTICLE?

An ARTICLE is a word placed before a noun to indicate   1
whether the noun refers to an unspecified person, animal,
place, thing, event, idea or to a particular person, animal,
etc. (see *What is a Noun?*, p. 7).

> I saw *a* boy in the street.
> |
> an unspecified boy

> I saw *the* boy you spoke about.
> |
> a particular boy

INDEFINITE ARTICLES
IN ENGLISH   10

An INDEFINITE ARTICLE is used before a noun when we are
not speaking of a particular person, animal, etc. There are
two indefinite articles, *a* and *an*.

A is used before a word beginning with a consonant.

> I saw *a* boy in the street. .
> |
> not a particular boy

An is used before a word beginning with a vowel.

> We visited *an* island in the Adriatic.   20
> |
> not a particular island

The indefinite article is used only with a singular noun.
With a plural noun, the word *some* may be used in place
of the indefinite article, but it is usually omitted (see *What
is Meant by Number?*, p. 13 and "Partitives," p. 18).

IN ITALIAN

As in English, an indefinite article is used before a noun
when it refers to an unspecified person, animal, etc. In
Italian, however, the indefinite article has different forms   30
because it must match the gender of the noun it modifies.
In order to select the proper form, you must consider
whether the noun is masculine or feminine (see *What is
Meant by Gender?*, p. 9). This "matching" is called AGREE-
MENT; one says that "the article *agrees* with the noun."

- **un** precedes a masculine singular noun

  | un libro | *a book* |
  | un esame | *an exam* |

- **uno** precedes a masculine singular noun beginning with a **z**- or an **s** + consonant

  | uno zio | *an uncle* |
  | uno studente | *a student* |

- **una** precedes a feminine singular noun

  | una casa | *a house* |
  | una ragazza | *a girl* |

- **un'** precedes a feminine singular noun beginning with a vowel

  | un' automobile | *an automobile* |
  | un' amica | *a girl friend* |

The indefinite article is used only with a singular noun; if the noun is plural, the partitive usually replaces it (see "Partitives," p. 18).

DEFINITE ARTICLES
IN ENGLISH

A **DEFINITE ARTICLE** is used before a noun when we are speaking about a particular person, animal, place, thing, event, or idea. There is one definite article, *the*.

I saw *the* boy you spoke about.

a particular boy

We visited *the* island you recommended.

a particular island

The definite article remains *the* when the noun becomes plural.

I saw *the* boys you spoke about.
We visited *the* islands you recommended.

IN ITALIAN

As in English, a definite article is used before a noun when referring to a particular person, animal, etc. In Italian, however, the definite article has different forms because it must match the gender and number of the noun it modifies. In order to select the proper form, you must consider whether the noun is masculine or feminine, singular or plural. This "matching" is called **AGREEMENT** (one says that "the article *agrees* with the noun").

- **il** precedes a masculine singular noun

il libro	*the book*
il ragazzo	*the boy*

- **lo** precedes a masculine singular noun beginning with a z- or an s + consonant-

lo zio	*the uncle*
lo studente	*the student*

- **la** precedes a feminine singular noun

la casa	*the house*
la ragazza	*the girl*

- **l'** precedes a masculine or feminine singular noun beginning with a vowel.

l'anno *m.*	*the year*
l'orologio *m.*	*the watch*
l'idea *f.*	*the idea*
l'alba *f.*	*the dawn*

- **i** precedes a masculine plural noun

i libri	*the books*
i ragazzi	*the boys*

- **gli** precedes a masculine plural noun beginning with either z- or s + consonant-, or a vowel

gli studenti	*the students*
gli anni	*the years*

- **le** precedes a feminine plural noun

le case	*the houses*
le albe	*the dawns*

Here is a chart you can use as reference:

Noun begins with:	INDEFINITE ARTICLES		DEFINITE ARTICLES			
	SINGULAR		SINGULAR		PLURAL	
	masc.	fem.	masc. sing.		masc.	sing.
1. vowel	un	un'	l'	l'	gli	le
2. z or s + consonant	uno	una	lo	la	gli	le
3. other consonant	un	una	il	la	i	le

CAREFUL — The definite article is used more frequently in Italian than in English. Compare the following Italian and English sentences.

La guerra è terribile.
War is terrible.

Quella donna è **la** signora Bianchi.
That woman is Mrs. Bianchi.

L'Italia acoglie bene **i** turisti.
Italy welcomes tourists.

Consult your Italian textbook to learn when to use the definite article in Italian.

PARTITIVES

A **PARTITIVE** indicates that only part of a whole *(some* bread, *some* water) or part of a group of things or people *(some* letters, *some* boys) is being referred to.

IN ENGLISH

The idea of the partitive is normally expressed with *some* or *any,* although these words are often dropped.

He is buying *(some)* bread.
She drank *(some)* water.

I saw *(some)* boys on the street.
I don't have *(any)* friends here.

IN ITALIAN

Partitives have a singular and a plural form. They are normally expressed by the word **di** + the definite article which agrees with the gender and number of the noun.

$$\text{di} + \begin{cases} \text{il} & \text{del} \\ \text{lo} & \text{dello} \\ \text{l'} & \text{dell'} \\ \text{la} & \text{della} \\ \text{i} & \text{dei} \\ \text{gli} & \text{degli} \\ \text{le} & \text{delle} \end{cases} \begin{array}{l} \text{SINGULAR} \\ \\ \text{PLURAL} \end{array}$$

NONCOUNT NOUNS — As the name implies, a noncount noun designates an object that cannot be counted and is, therefore, always singular. For example, the noun *water* is a noncount noun because it cannot be preceded by a number. (You cannot count *one water, two waters,* etc.) As a singular noun, it can only be preceded by a singular form of the partitive.

Compra **del** pane.
        |
     di + il
*He is buying (**some**) bread.*

Ha bevuto **dell'**acqua.   160

       |
    di + l'

She drank (some) water.

COUNT NOUNS — Count nouns are people or things which can be counted. For example, the nouns *boy, class, book* can be preceded by a number (*one* boy, *two* boys, etc.). The plural forms of the partitive are only used with count nouns.

Ho visto **dei** ragazzi per strada.

       |
    di + i   170

I saw (some) boys on the street.

Compra **delle** pere.

      |
    di + le

He is buying (some) pears.

CAREFUL — Although the partitive words *some* or *any* may be omitted in English, the partitive is normally used in Italian. It is optional, however, in interrogative sentences (see *What are Declarative and Interrogative Sentences?*, p. 44) and is never used in negative sentences (see *What are Affirmative and Negative Sentences?*, p. 42).   180

Hai **(del)** pane? No, non ho pane.

Do you have (any) bread? No, I don't have (any) bread.

Hai **(degli)** amici in Italia? No, non ho amici.

Do you have (any) friends in Italy? No, I don't have (any) friends.

CHAPTER

6

WHAT IS THE POSSESSIVE?

1   The term POSSESSIVE indicates that one noun owns or pos-
sesses, or has a relationship to, another noun (see *What is a
Noun?*, p. 7).

The *teacher's* book is on the desk.

noun   noun
possessor possessed

Aunt Laura is my *mother's* sister.

IN ENGLISH

You can show possession in one of two ways:

10   1. with an apostrophe — In this structure, the noun possessor comes before the noun possessed.

- a singular common or proper noun possessor adds an
  apostrophe + "s"

John's shirt
the *girl's* dress

singular possessor

- a plural possessor ending with "s" adds an apostrophe

the *girls'* father
20   the *boys'* team

plural possessor

- a plural possessor not ending with "s" adds an apostrophe + "s"

the *children's* playground
the *men's* team

plural possessor

2. with the word "of"—In this structure, the noun possessed comes before the noun possessor.

30   - a singular or plural common noun possessor is preceded by *of the* or *of a*

the book *of the professor*
the branches *of a tree*

singular common noun possessor

- a proper noun possessor is preceded by *of*
  the dress *of Mary*

  proper noun possessor

IN ITALIAN

40

There is only one way to express possession and that is by using the equivalent of the "of" construction (2. above). The apostrophe structure does not exist.

To express possession the following structure is used: the noun possessed + **di** *of* + (definite article) + the noun possessor. (To see how **di** combines with definite articles see p. 18.)

John's shirt	*the shirt of John*
	la camicia **di Giovanni**
the girl's dress	*the dress of the girl*
	il vestito **della ragazza**
	di + la
the boy's shirt	*the shirt of the boy*
	la camicia **del ragazzo**
	di + il
the girls' father	*the father of the girls*
	il padre **delle ragazze**
	di + le
the boys' team	*the team of the boys*
	la squadra **dei ragazzi**
	di + i

50

60

CHAPTER

7

WHAT IS A VERB?

A **VERB** is a word that indicates a physical or mental activity or condition.

IN ENGLISH

Let us look at different types of words which are verbs:

- a physical activity to run, to talk, to walk
- a mental activity   to hope, to dream, to think
- a condition   to be, to seem, to have

To help you learn to recognize verbs, here is a paragraph where the verbs are in italics:

> The three students *entered* the restaurant, *selected* a table, *hung* up their coats and *sat* down. They *looked* at the menu and *asked* the waitress what she *recommended*. She *advised* the daily special, beef stew. It *was* not expensive. They *chose* a bottle of red wine and *ordered* a salad. The service *was* slow, but the food *tasted* excellent. Good cooking, they *decided, takes* time. They *ordered* pastry for dessert and *finished* the meal with coffee.

The verb is one of the most important words in a sentence. You cannot write a **COMPLETE SENTENCE** (i.e., express a complete thought) without a verb. It is important that you learn to identify verbs because the function of many words in a sentence often depends on their relationship to the verb. For instance, the subject of a sentence performs the action of the verb and the object receives the action of the verb (see *What is a Subject?*, p. 28 and *What is an Object?*, p. 117).

IN ITALIAN

Verbs are identified the same way that they are in English.

TERMS USED TO TALK ABOUT VERBS

Infinitive — The dictionary form, i.e, the name of the verb, is called an infinitive: *to eat, to sleep, to drink* (see *What is an Infinitive?*, p. 24).

Conjugation — A verb is conjugated or changes its form to reflect the subject, tense, mood: *I do, he does, we did* (see *What is a Verb Conjugation?*, p. 35).

Tense — A verb indicates tense, that is the time (present, past, or future) of the action: *I am, I was, I will be* (see *What is Meant by Tense?*, p. 49).

Mood — A verb shows mood, that is, the speakers' attitude toward what they are saying (see *What is Meant by Mood?*, p. 47).

Voice — A verb shows voice, that is, the relation between the subject and the action of the verb (see *What is Meant by Active and Passive Voice?*, p. 89).

Auxiliary verb — A verb used to form tenses of another verb (see *What is an Auxiliary Verb?*, p. 26).

Participle — A verb form often used with an auxiliary verb to form a tense (see *What is a Participle?*, p. 57).

Transitive or Intransitive — A verb can be classified as transitive or intransitive depending on whether or not the verb can take a direct object (see p. 118 in *What is an Object?*).

WHAT IS AN INFINITIVE?

An INFINITIVE is the name of the verb (see *What is a Verb?*, p. 22).

IN ENGLISH

The infinitive is composed of two words: *to* + the dictionary form of the verb: *to speak, to dance,* etc. By DICTIONARY FORM, we mean the form of the verb that is listed as the entry in the dictionary: *speak, dance.* The infinitive can never be used as the main verb of a sentence; there must always be a conjugated verb form with it.

Carlo and Silvia want *to dance* together.
          main verb infinitive

It started *to rain.*
main verb infinitive

To learn is exciting.
infinitive main verb

The dictionary form alone is used after verbs such as *must, can, will, may, might,* etc.

Paolo must *be* home by noon.
      dictionary form

I can *swim.*
    dictionary form

IN ITALIAN

The infinitive is composed of only one word which ends in **-are, -ere,** or **-ire**; these are called the INFINITIVE ENDINGS.

cant**are**	*to sing*
vend**ere**	*to sell*
part**ire**	*to leave*

The initial part of the infinitive, called THE STEM, carries the meaning of the word.

cant-are   *to sing*
sing to

The infinitive is used after any conjugated verb other than **essere** *to be,* **avere** *to have,* or **stare** *to be.* See *What is a Verb Conjugation?*, p. 35.

Giovanni e Maria vogliono **ballare** insieme.

conjugated infinitive
verb

*John and Mary want **to dance** together.*

Cominciò a **piovere.**

conjugated infinitive
verb

*It started **to rain.***

So **nuotare.**

  infinitive
conjugated
verb

*I can **swim.***

Dovresti **studiare** di più.

conjugated infinitive
verb

*You should **study** more.*

Notice that in the last two examples English uses the dictionary form and Italian uses the infinitive.

CAREFUL — In English it is possible to change the meaning of a verb by placing short words (prepositions or adverbs) after it. For example, the verb *look* in Column A below changes meaning depending on the word that follows.

Column A

to look *for*	I *am looking for* a book. *[to search for]*
to look *after*	I *look after* children. *[to take care of]*
to look *into*	He will *look into* the matter. *[to investigate]*
to look *at*	*Look at* that car. *[to observe]*

In Italian, however, it is not possible to change the meaning of a verb by adding a preposition or an adverb. An entirely different verb is used to reflect the various meanings. All the examples under Column A above will be found under the dictionary entry *look.* However, don't make the mistake of selecting the first entry under *look* **guardare** and adding **per** *for* or **dopo** *after;* the result is meaningless in Italian. You will have to search the entire dictionary entry under *look* for the correct combination of words that will give you the Italian equivalent.

to look for	cercare
to look after	badare
to look into	investigare, approfondire

CHAPTER

9

WHAT IS AN AUXILIARY VERB?

A verb is called an AUXILIARY VERB or HELPING VERB when it helps another verb form one of its tenses. It can also be used alone, in which case it is called the MAIN VERB.

Mary is a writer.	is	MAIN VERB
Mary is writing a novel.	is	AUXILIARY VERB
Paul has many friends.	has	MAIN VERB
Paul has invited his friends.	has	AUXILIARY VERB

A verb tense composed of an auxiliary verb plus a main verb is called a COMPOUND TENSE; a verb tense composed of only the main verb is called a SIMPLE TENSE.

IN ENGLISH

There are three auxiliary verbs: *to have, to be,* and *to do,* as well as a series of "helping" words which indicate either the tense *(will, would, used to)* or a mood *(may, might)* of the main verb. (See *What is Meant by Tense?,* p. 49 and *What is Meant by Mood?,* p. 47.)

Mary *has* read a book.   PAST TENSE
  auxiliary *to have*

May *used to* read a lot.   PAST TENSE (HABITUAL)
  auxiliary *used to*

Mary *will* read a book.   FUTURE TENSE
  auxiliary *will*

May the best man win.   SUBJUNCTIVE MOOD
  auxiliary *may*

The auxiliary verb *to do* is used to formulate questions and to make sentences negative (see *What are Declarative and Interrogative Sentences?,* p. 44 and *What are Affirmative and Negative Sentences?,* p. 42).

Does Mary read novels?   INTERROGATIVE SENTENCE
Mary *does not* read novels.   NEGATIVE SENTENCE

IN ITALIAN

There are two verbs that can be used as auxiliary verbs **avere** *to have* and **essere** *to be.* As in English, they are used to form tenses and moods of the main verb (see *What is Meant by Tense?,* p. 49, and *What is a Past Tense?,* p. 62).

Avere and **essere** are most frequently found as main verbs (see *What are Some Equivalents of "To be"?*, p. 52).

Il ragazzo **ha** una mela.   40

      main verb **avere** *to have*

The boy *has* an apple.

Il ragazzo **ha** mangiato la mela.

      auxiliary verb   main verb
      avere

The boy *has* eaten the apple.

La ragazza **è** al cinema.

      main verb **essere** *to be*

The girl *is* at the movies.   50

La ragazza **è** andata al cinema.

      auxiliary verb   main verb
      essere

The girl *has* gone to the movies.

CAREFUL — Since the auxiliary *do* and its forms *(does, did)*, as well as the "helping" words *(will, would, used to, may, might)* do not exist as separate words in Italian, do not translate them as such. Their meaning is conveyed by a single conjugated verb form.

WHAT IS A SUBJECT?

In a sentence the person or thing that performs the action is called the **SUBJECT**.[1] When you wish to find the subject of a sentence, always look for the verb first; then ask *who?* or *what?* before the verb. The answer will be the subject.

> John speaks Italian.
> QUESTION: *Who* speaks Italian? ANSWER: John.
> *John* is the singular subject.
> Are John and Mary coming tonight?
> QUESTION: *Who* is coming tonight? ANSWER: John and Mary.
> *John and Mary* is the plural subject.
> Are the keys on the table?
> QUESTION: *What* is on the table? ANSWER: The keys.
> *The keys* is the plural subject.

Train yourself to always ask the question to find the subject. Never assume a word is the subject because it comes first in the sentence. Subjects can be in many different places of a sentence as you can see in the following examples in which the **subject** is in boldface and the *verb* italicized:

> *Did* **the game** *start* on time?
> After playing for two hours, **Marco** *became* exhausted.
> Looking in the mirror *was* a little **girl**.

Some sentences have more than one main verb; you have to find the subject of each verb.

> **The boys** *were cooking* while **Anna** *was setting* the table.
> *Boys* is the plural subject of *were cooking*.
> *Anna* is the singular subject of *was setting*.

In English and in Italian it is very important to identify the subject of each verb and then select the verb form which corresponds to that subject. (See *What is a Verb Conjugation?*, p. 35.)

---

[1]The subject performs the action of the verb in an active sentence, but is acted upon in a passive sentence (see *What is Meant by Active and Passive Voice?*, p. 89).

11

WHAT IS A PRONOUN?

A **PRONOUN** is a word used in place of one or more nouns. It may stand, therefore, for a person, animal, place, thing, event, or idea (see *What is a Noun?*, p. 7).

For instance, instead of repeating the proper noun "Lisa" in the following two sentences, it is natural to use a pronoun in the second sentence:

> *Lisa* likes to sing. *Lisa* goes to practice every day.
> *Lisa* likes to sing. *She* goes to practice every day.

A pronoun can only be used to refer to someone or something that has already been mentioned. The noun replaced by the pronoun is called the **ANTECEDENT**. In the example above, the noun *Lisa* is the antecedent of the pronoun *she*.

IN ENGLISH

There are different types of pronouns. They are studied in separate sections of this handbook. Below we will simply list the most important categories and refer you to the section where they are discussed.

Subject pronouns (see p. 31)

> *I* go.
> *They* read.

Direct object pronouns (see p. 124)

> Carlo loves *her*.
> Laura saw *them* at the theater.

Indirect object pronouns (see p. 126)

> The boy wrote *me* the letter.
> Carlo gave *us* the book.

Object of preposition pronouns (see p. 128)

> Paolo is going to the movies with *us*.
> He did it for *her*.

Stressed (disjunctive) pronouns (see p. 130)

> I saw *her*, not *him*.
> I only sent *them* flowers.

Reflexive pronouns — used with reflexive verbs (see p. 86)

> I cut *myself*.
> We washed *ourselves*.

Interrogative pronouns — used in questions (see p. 132)

> *Who* is that young man?
>
> *What* do you want?

Demonstrative pronouns — used to point out persons or things (see p. 137)

> *This (one)* is expensive. *That (one)* is cheap.

Possessive pronouns — used to show possession (see p. 140)

> Whose book is that? *Mine. Yours* is on the table.

Relative pronouns — used to introduce relative subordinate clauses (see p. 142)

> The man *who* came is very nice.
>
> Marco, *whom* you met, is the president of the company.

IN ITALIAN

Pronouns are identified in the same way as in English. In Italian a pronoun usually agrees in gender and number with its antecedent.

WHAT IS A SUBJECT PRONOUN?

A **SUBJECT PRONOUN** is a pronoun used as a subject of a verb   1
(see *What is a Subject?*, p. 28 and *What is a Pronoun?*, p. 29).

> He worked while she read.
>> QUESTION: Who worked? ANSWER: He.
>> *He* is the subject of the verb *worked*.
>
>> QUESTION: Who read? ANSWER: She.
>> *She* is the subject of the verb *read*.

Subject pronouns are classified as follows: the person
speaking, the **FIRST PERSON**, the person spoken to, the **SECOND
PERSON**, or the person spoken about, the **THIRD PERSON**. These
are further divided according to whether one person (sin-   10
gular) or more than one person (plural) is involved. The term
"person" in the grammatical sense does not necessarily
mean a human being, it can refer to anyone or anything.

Let us compare the subject pronouns of English and Italian.

	ENGLISH	ITALIAN	
SINGULAR			
1ˢᵗ person *the person speaking*	I	**io**	
2ⁿᵈ person *the person spoken to*	you	**tu** [familiar] **Lei** [formal]	20
3ʳᵈ person *the person or object spoken about*	{ he she it	**lui** **lei**	
PLURAL			
1ˢᵗ person *the person speaking plus others* *John* and *I* speak Italian. we	we	**noi**	
2ⁿᵈ person *the persons spoken to* *Anita* and *you* speak Italian. you	you	**voi** [familiar] **Loro** [formal]	30
3ʳᵈ person *the persons or objects spoken about* *John* and *Anita* speak Italian. they	they	**loro** [only persons]	

As you can see from the chart, there is not an exact correspondence between English and Italian subject pronouns. Let us look at *it, they* and *you.*

"IT" AND "THEY"
IN ENGLISH

Since a subject pronoun must always be used with every verb form, *it* is used when referring to a thing or an idea, and *they* when referring to more than one thing or idea.

> *He* has a new car. *It* is a Ferrari.
> *She* has many records. *They* are all new.

IN ITALIAN

The subject pronouns are used far less frequently than in English (see p. 40). Especially *it* and *they* referring to things are almost never used and should not be translated.

> *John has a new car. **It is** a Ferrari.*
> > *It* is understood as part of the verb è.
> > Giovanni ha una macchina nuova. È una Ferrari.

> *Maria has many records. **They are** all new.*
> > *They* is understood as part of the verb **sono**.
> > Maria ha molti dischi. **Sono** tutti nuovi.

"YOU" — TU, LEI, VOI, LORO
IN ENGLISH

You is the only pronoun of address. It is used when speaking to anyone, a close friend or a stranger. For instance, *you* is appropriate whether you are addressing the President of the United States or a member of your family.

> Do *you* have any questions, Mr. President?
> Johnny, *you* must eat your spinach!

Also, *you* is used whether you are addressing one person or many people. For example, if there are many people standing in a room and you ask: "Are *you* coming with me?" the *you* could be interpreted as an invitation to one person or to more than one.

IN ITALIAN

As you can see from the chart on p. 31, there are two sets of pronouns for *you*. **Tu** and **voi** are called FAMILIAR YOU used with close friends, relatives and children and **Lei** and **Loro** are called FORMAL YOU used with persons you do not know well.

Each of these has a singular form if you are addressing one person and a plural form if you are addressing more than one.

Familiar "you" → **tu** or **voi**

The familiar forms of *you* are used with members of one's family, friends, children and pets. In general, the familiar *you* is used with persons you call by first name.

1. to address one person (singular) → **tu**

   Maria, **tu** vieni con me?
   *Mary, are **you** coming with me?*

2. to address more than one person (plural) → **voi**

   Giovanni e Maria, **voi** venite con me?
   *John and Mary, are **you** coming with me?*

Formal "you" → **Lei** or **Loro**

The forms of formal *you* are used to address someone you do not know well or to whom you wish to show respect. In general, the formal *you* is used with persons you address with a title: Miss Smith, Mr. Jones, Dr. Anderson. **Lei** and **Loro**, are always written with a capital letter.

1. to address one person (singular) → **Lei**

   Signor Rossi, **Lei** viene con me?
   *Mr. Rossi, are **you** coming with me?*

2. to address more than one person (plural) → **Loro**

   Signori Rossi, **Loro** vengono con me?
   *Mr. and Mrs. Rossi, are **you** coming with me?*

Here are the steps to find the appropriate form of *you*:

1. FAMILIAR OR FORMAL — Is the familiar or formal form appropriate?
2. NUMBER — Is one or more persons being addressed?
3. SELECTION — Select the proper form after completing steps 1 and 2.

Let's find the Italian equivalent for *you* in the following sentences.

> *John, are **you** coming with me?*
>   1. FAMILIAR OR FORMAL: John → familiar
>   2. NUMBER: one person → singular
>   3. SELECTION: **tu**
> Giovanni, **tu** vieni con me?
>
> *Mario and Gloria, are **you** coming with me?*
>   1. FAMILIAR OR FORMAL: Mario and Gloria → familiar
>   2. NUMBER: two persons → plural
>   3. SELECTION: **voi**
> Mario e Gloria, **voi** venite con me?

*Mr. President, are **you** coming with me?*
    1. FAMILIAR OR FORMAL: Mr. President → formal
    2. NUMBER: one person → singular
    3. SELECTION: **Lei**
Signor Presidente, **Lei** viene con me?

*Mr. and Mrs. Casa, are **you** coming with me?*
    1. FAMILIAR OR FORMAL: Mr. and Mrs. Casa → formal
    2. NUMBER: two persons → plural
    3. SELECTION: **Loro**
Signori Casa, **Loro** vengono con me?

130   As you can see, the English question "Are *you* coming with me?" may be expressed in four different ways in Italian and the choice of the appropriate form of *you* has an important social meaning. If you are in doubt regarding the selection of the formal or familiar mode of address, use the formal **Lei, Loro**, since the improper use of the familiar **tu, voi** would be considered rude.

It is also important to note that the selection of the familiar or formal pronoun will determine the form of the verb to be used (see *What is a Verb Conjugation?*, p. 35).

WHAT IS A VERB CONJUGATION?

A **VERB CONJUGATION** is a list of the six possible forms of the 1
verb for a particular tense. For every tense, there is a different
verb form for each of the six persons used as the subject of
the verb. In this section we shall limit ourselves to the present tense (see *What is Meant by Tense?*, p. 49 and *What is a
Subject?*, p. 28).

IN ENGLISH

Most verbs change very little. Let us look at the various
forms of the verb *to sing* when each of the possible pronouns is the performer of the action. 10

> **SINGULAR**
> 1ˢᵗ **person**   I *sing* with the music.
> 2ⁿᵈ **person**   You *sing* with the music.
>
> 3ʳᵈ **person**   { He *sings* with the music.
>   She *sings* with the music.
>   It *sings* with the music.
>
> **PLURAL**
> 1ˢᵗ **person**   We *sing* with the music.
> 2ⁿᵈ **person**   You *sing* with the music.
> 3ʳᵈ **person**   They *sing* with the music. 20

Conjugating in the present tense is relatively easy because
there is only one change in the verb forms: in the 3ʳᵈ
person singular the verb adds an "-s".

The English verb that changes the most is the verb *to be*
which has three different verb forms in the present: *I am,
you are, he, she* or *it is, we are, you are, they are.*

IN ITALIAN

For every tense of a verb, there are six different verb forms
corresponding to each of the six persons used as the sub- 30
ject (see p. 31). Learning six forms for every verb would be
an endless task. Fortunately, most Italian verbs are regular
verbs.

REGULAR VERBS are verbs whose forms follow a regular pattern. Only one example must be memorized and the pattern can then be applied to other verbs of the same group.

IRREGULAR VERBS are verbs whose forms do not follow a regular pattern and must be memorized individually.

SUBJECT

Let us now conjugate the verb **cantare** *to sing* in the present tense paying special attention to the subject pronoun.

SINGULAR

1ˢᵗ person	io	canto
2ⁿᵈ person	tu	canti
3ʳᵈ person	{ lui / lei / Lei }	canta

PLURAL

1ˢᵗ person	noi	cantiamo
2ⁿᵈ person	voi	cantate
3ʳᵈ person	{ loro / Loro }	cantano

Each subject represents the doer of the action of the verb.

1ˢᵗ person singular — The "*I* form" of the verb (the **io** form) is used whenever the person speaking is the doer of the action.

> Generalmente **io canto** molto bene.
> *Normally, **I sing** very well.*

2ⁿᵈ person singular — The "*you* familiar form" of the verb (the **tu** form) is used whenever the person spoken to (with whom you are on familiar terms) is the doer of the action (see pp. 32-4 in *What is a Subject Pronoun?*).

> Giovanni, **tu canti** molto bene.
> *John, **you sing** very well.*

3ʳᵈ person singular — The "*he, she, you* formal form" of the verb is used with many possible subjects.

1. the third person singular masculine pronoun **lui** *he* and the third person singular feminine pronoun **lei** *she*

> **Lui canta** molto bene.
> *He sings very well.*
> **Lei canta** molto bene.
> *She sings very well.*

2. the singular pronoun **Lei** (formal *you*)

> Signorina Dini, **Lei canta** molto bene.
> *Miss Dini, **you sing** very well.*

3. one proper name

> Maria **canta** molto bene.
> *Mary **sings** very well.*

80

4. a singular noun

> Il ragazzo **canta** molto bene.
> *The boy **sings** very well.*
>
> L'uccello **canta** molto bene.
> *The bird **sings** very well.*

The subject pronoun *it* has no equivalent in Italian. *It* as a subject is almost never expressed.

> *John has a Ferrari. **It is** very beautiful.*
> Giovanni ha una Ferrari. È molto bella.

90

It is understood as the subject of the verb è.

1ˢᵗ person plural — The *"we* form" of the verb (the **noi** form) is used whenever "I" (the speaker) is one of the doers of the action; that is, whenever the speaker is included in a plural or multiple subject.

> Io, Isabella, e Gloria **cantiamo** molto bene.
>   **noi**
> *Isabella, Gloria and I **sing** very well.*
>
>> In this sentence *Isabella, Gloria and I* could be replaced by the pronoun *we,* so that in Italian you must use the **noi** form of the verb.

100

2ⁿᵈ person plural — The *"you* familiar plural form" of the verb (the **voi** form) is used when you are speaking to two or more persons with whom you would use **tu** individually.

> Tu, Maria e Susanna **cantate** molto bene.
>   **voi**
> *Mary, Susan and you **sing** very well.*
>
>> In this sentence *Mary and Susan and you* (whom you would address individually with the **tu** form) could be replaced by the pronoun *you* **voi,** so that in Italian you must use the **voi** form of the verb.

110

3ʳᵈ person plural — The *"they* form" of the verb (the **loro** form) is used with many possible subjects.

1. the third person plural pronoun **loro** *they*

> **Loro cantano** molto bene.
> *They **sing** very well.*

2. the plural pronoun **Loro** (formal *you*)

> Signori Casa, **Loro cantano** molto bene.
> *Mr. and Mrs. Casa, **you sing** very well.*

120

3. two or more names

Isabella, Gloria e Roberto **cantano** molto bene.

          loro

Isabella, Gloria and Robert sing very well.

> In this sentence *Isabella, Gloria and Robert* could be replaced by *they* so that in Italian you must use the **loro** form of the verb.

4. two or more singular nouns

La ragazza e suo padre **cantano** molto bene.

          loro

The girl and her father sing very well.

> In this sentence *the girl and her father* could be replaced by *they* so that in Italian you must use the **loro** form of the verb.

5. a plural noun

Le ragazze **cantano** molto bene.
The girls sing very well.

The subject pronoun *they* referring to things is almost never expressed.

> *Mary has a nice pair of shoes.* **They are** *from Florence.*
> Maria ha un bel paio di scarpe. **Sono** di Firenze.
>
> *They* is understood as the subject of the verb **sono**.

VERB FORM

Let us again look at the conjugation of the present tense of **cantare** *to sing* paying special attention to the forms of the verb. Each of the six persons has a different ending, corresponding to a different subject pronoun. Note, however, that the 3rd person singular form, **canta**, has three possible subject pronouns: **lui** *he*, **lei** *she*, **Lei** (formal *you*) and the 3rd person plural has two possible subjects pronouns: **loro** *they* and **Loro** (formal *you*).

SINGULAR

1st person	io	canto
2nd person	tu	canti
3rd person	{ lui / lei / Lei }	canta

PLURAL

1st person	noi	cant**iamo**
2nd person	voi	cant**ate**
3rd person	{ loro / Loro }	cant**ano**

The Italian verb is composed of two parts.

1. The STEM (also called the ROOT) is found by dropping the infinitive endings (see *What is an Infinitive?*, p. 24).

INFINITIVE	STEM
cant**are**	cant-
tem**ere**	tem-
apr**ire**	apr-

The stem usually does not change throughout a conjugation.   170

2. The ENDING changes for each person and for each tense in the conjugation of regular and irregular verbs. In order to choose the correct endings, you need to know to which group the verb belongs.

VERB GROUPS

Regular verbs are divided into three groups, also called CONJUGATIONS. The groups are identified according to the infinitive endings.   180

1ST CONJUGATION	2ND CONJUGATION	3RD CONJUGATION
-are	-ere	-ire

Each of the three verb groups has its own set of endings for each tense. You will need to memorize the forms of only one sample verb from each group in order to conjugate any regular verb belonging to that group. As an example, let us look more closely at regular verbs of the first conjugation, that is, verbs like **cantare** *to sing*, **parlare** *to speak* or **imparare** *to learn* which have the same infinitive ending -**are**. Here are the endings added to the verb   190 stem to form the present tense (see *What is the Present Tense?*, p. 51).

SUBJECT	ENDING
io	-o
tu	-i
lui / lei / Lei	-a
noi	-iamo
voi	-ate
loro / Loro	-ano

   200

After you have memorized the endings for a verb such as **cantare**, you can then conjugate any regular **-are** verb by following these steps.

1. CONJUGATION — Identify the conjugation of the verb by its infinitive ending.

    -are or first conjugation

2. STEM — Find the verb stem.

parl**are**	→	parl-
impar**are**	→	impar-

3. ENDING — Add the ending that agrees with the subject.

SUBJECT	VERB FORM	VERB FORM
io	parl**o**	impar**o**
tu	parl**i**	impar**i**
lui lei Lei	parl**a**	impar**a**
noi	parl**iamo**	impar**iamo**
voi	parl**ate**	impar**ate**
loro Loro	parl**ano**	impar**ano**

The endings for regular **-ere** and **-ire** verbs will be different, but the three steps are the same.

MEMORIZING CONJUGATIONS

It will be easier for you to memorize the conjugation of regular and irregular verbs if you follow these steps:

1. Look for a pattern within the conjugation of the verb itself: which stems and endings are similar or how do the other forms differ.

2. As you learn new tenses of a verb, look for similarities and differences in the stem and endings with the tense(s) of that verb you've already learned.

3. As you learn new verbs, look for similarities and differences in the stem and endings with the conjugation of the verbs you've already learned.

OMITTING THE SUBJECT PRONOUN

As you can see, the Italian verb ending indicates the subject. For instance, "parlo" can only have **io** as a subject. Similarly, the subject of "parli" can only be **tu**, the subject of "parliamo" **noi**, and the subject of "parlate" **voi**. Since you know the subject from the verb form, the subject pronoun is usually omitted.

parlo	*I speak*
parli	*you speak*
parl**iamo**	*we speak*
parl**ate**	*you speak*

Subject pronouns are only used to clarify the subject or to add emphasis.   250

- to clarify the subject in the 3rd person

parla $\left\{\begin{array}{ll} \textbf{lui} \text{ parla} & \textit{he speaks} \\ \textbf{lei} \text{ parla} & \textit{she speaks} \\ \textbf{Lei} \text{ parla} & \textit{you speak} \end{array}\right.$

parlano $\left\{\begin{array}{ll} \textbf{loro} \text{ parlano} & \textit{they speak} \\ \textbf{Loro} \text{ parlano} & \textit{you speak} \end{array}\right.$

- to emphasize the subject

io canto	*I sing* [but *he* doesn't]
noi cantiamo	*we sing* [but *they* don't] 260

CAREFUL — Remember that when the subject pronouns *it* and *they* refer to things they are almost never expressed in Italian.

WHAT ARE AFFIRMATIVE AND
NEGATIVE SENTENCES?

A sentence can be classified as to whether the information it contains is stated in a positive or negative way.

An **AFFIRMATIVE SENTENCE** states in a positive way the information it contains; it *affirms* the information.

> John works in a factory.
> Italy is a country in Europe.
> They like to travel.

A **NEGATIVE SENTENCE** does not state in a positive way the information it contains; it *negates* the information.

> John does *not* work in a shoe store.
> Italy is *not* a country in Asia.
> They do *not* like to travel by bus.

IN ENGLISH

An affirmative sentence can become a negative sentence in one of two ways:

1. by adding the word *not* after forms of the verb *to be* and auxiliary verbs such as *can, may, have* (see *What is an Auxiliary Verb?*, p. 26)

AFFIRMATIVE	→	**N**EGATIVE
John is a student.		John is *not* a student.
Mary can do it.		Mary can*not* do it.
They will travel.		They will *not* travel.

Frequently, *not* is attached to the verb and the letter "o" is replaced by an apostrophe; this new word is called a **CONTRACTION.**

> John *isn't* a student.
> is not

> Mary *can't* do it.
> cannot

> They *won't* travel.
> will not

Note that the contraction of *will not* is *won't.*

2. by adding the auxiliary verb *do, does,* or *did* + *not* + the dictionary form of the main verb. *Do* or *does* is used for

negatives in the present tense and *did* for negatives in the past tense. (See *What is the Present Tense?*, p. 51 and *What is a Past Tense?*, p. 62.)

AFFIRMATIVE	→	NEGATIVE
We study a lot.		We *do not study* a lot.
Julia writes well.		Julia *does not write* well.
The train arrived.		The train *did not arrive.*

Frequently *do, does,* or *did* form a contraction with *not*: *don't, doesn't,* or *didn't.*

A negative sentence can also be formed with negative words such as *no, nobody, nothing, never* (see *What are Positive and Negative Indefinites?*, p. 151).

IN ITALIAN

The basic rule for turning an affirmative sentence into a negative sentence is simpler than in English. You normally place the word **non** in front of the conjugated verb.

AFFIRMATIVE	→	NEGATIVE
Studiamo molto.		**Non** studiamo molto.
We study a lot.		*We **do not** study a lot.*
Giulia scrive bene.		Giulia **non** scrive bene.
Julia writes well.		*Julia **does not** write well.*
Il treno è arrivato.		Il treno **non** è arrivato.
The train arrived.		*The train **did not** arrive.*

As in English, negative sentences can be formed in Italian with negative words such as **nessuno** *nobody,* **niente** *nothing,* **mai** *never.*

CAREFUL — Since there is no equivalent in Italian for the auxiliary forms *do, does* or *did*, you must omit them when forming a negative sentence.

WHAT ARE DECLARATIVE AND INTERROGATIVE SENTENCES?

A sentence can be classified according to its purpose, that is, whether it makes a statement or asks a question.

A **DECLARATIVE SENTENCE** is a sentence that is a statement; it *declares* the information.

> Rome is the capital of Italy.

An **INTERROGATIVE SENTENCE** is a sentence that asks a question.

> Is Rome the capital of Italy?

There are two types of questions based on the type of answer expected.

- yes-no questions — a "yes" or "no" answer is expected.

> Are you happy? Yes, I am. No, I am not.

- information questions — some information is expected. These questions start with word such as *who, what, which, why, when, where* (see *What is an Interrogative Pronoun?*, p. 132 and *What is an Interrogative Adjective?*, p. 105).

> When will he sing at La Scala? Next fall.

In written language, an interrogative sentence always ends with a question mark.

IN ENGLISH

A declarative sentence can be changed into an interrogative sentence in one of two ways:

1. by adding the auxiliary verb *do, does*, or *did* before the subject and changing the main verb to the dictionary form of the verb *(do* and *does* are used to introduce a question in the present tense and *did* to introduce a question in the past tense — see *What is the Present Tense?*, p. 51 and *What is a Past Tense?*, p. 62).

DECLARATIVE	→	INTERROGATIVE
The girls *study* together.		*Do* the girls *study* together?
Anna *likes* opera.		*Does* Anna *like* opera?
Paolo and Carlo *left*.		*Did* Paolo and Carlo *leave*?

2. by inverting or switching the normal word order of subject + verb so that the word order in the question is verb + subject. This is only used with forms of the verb *to be* and auxiliary verbs such as *will, may, can*, etc.

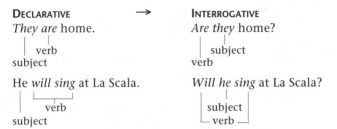

DECLARATIVE	→	INTERROGATIVE
They are home.		*Are they* home?

⁴⁰

He will sing at La Scala.   *Will he sing* at La Scala?

IN ITALIAN

A declarative sentence can be changed into an interrogative sentence by inversion, that is, by placing the subject after the verb.

⁵⁰

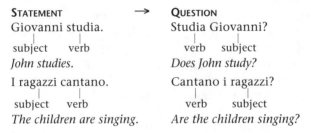

STATEMENT	→	QUESTION
Giovanni studia.		Studia Giovanni?
John studies.		*Does John study?*
I ragazzi cantano.		Cantano i ragazzi?
The children are singing.		*Are the children singing?*

When a statement consists of a subject and verb plus one or two words, those few words, referred to as the **REMAINDER,** are usually placed between them. The word order of the question is verb + remainder + subject.

⁶⁰

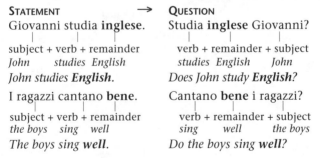

STATEMENT	→	QUESTION
Giovanni studia **inglese**.		Studia **inglese** Giovanni?
subject + verb + remainder		verb + remainder + subject
John studies English		*studies English John*
*John studies **English**.*		*Does John study **English**?*
I ragazzi cantano **bene**.		Cantano **bene** i ragazzi?
subject + verb + remainder		verb + remainder + subject
the boys sing well		*sing well the boys*
*The boys sing **well**.*		*Do the boys sing **well**?*

⁷⁰

CAREFUL — The verbs *do, does, did* used to form questions in English have no equivalent in Italian and are to be ignored in the formulation of a question.

TAG QUESTIONS

In English and in Italian you can also transform a statement into a question by adding a short phrase at the end of the statement. This short phrase is called a **TAG** or **TAG QUESTION**.

⁸⁰

IN ENGLISH

The tag question is determined by whether the statement is affirmative or negative.

- statement affirmative → the tag question negative

    John *is* a nice guy, *isn't he?*
    She *had* fun, *didn't she?*

- statement negative→ the tag question affirmative

    John *isn't* a nice guy, *is he?*
    She *didn't have* fun, *did she?*

90

The end part of the statement *(isn't he, is he)* is the tag or tag question.

IN ITALIAN

The choice of tag question is limited.

- statement affirmative → add **vero?**, **è vero?**, **no?**, or **non è vero?**

    Giovanni è un bravo ragazzo, **vero?**
    Giovanni è un bravo ragazzo, **è vero?**
    Giovanni è un bravo ragazzo, **no?**
    Giovanni è un bravo ragazzo, **non è vero?**
    *John is a nice guy, **isn't he?***

100

- statement negative→ only **vero?** or **è vero?** are possible

    Giovanni non è un bravo ragazzo, **vero?**
    Giovanni non è un bravo ragazzo, **è vero?**
    *John isn't a nice guy, **is he?***

WHAT IS MEANT BY MOOD?

Verbs can be conjugated in different **MOODS** which, in turn, are subdivided into one or more tenses (see *What is Meant by Tense?*, p. 49). The word "mood" is a variation of the word *mode* meaning manner or way. The various grammatical moods indicate the attitude of the speaker toward what he or she is saying.

IN ENGLISH

Verbs can be in one of three moods.

Indicative — The indicative mood is used to *indicate* facts. This is the most common mood, and most of the verb forms that you use in everyday conversation belong to the indicative mood.

> Robert *studies* Italian.
>
> present indicative
>
> Anita *was* here.
>
> past indicative
>
> They *will arrive* tomorrow.
>
> future indicative

Imperative — The imperative mood is used to give commands (see *What is the Imperative?*, p. 75). This mood is not divided into tenses.

> Robert, *study* Italian now!
> Anita, *be* home on time!

Subjunctive — The subjunctive is used not to indicate facts, but rather to express an attitude or feeling toward an event. Since this mood stresses feelings about a fact or an idea, it is "subjective" about them (see *What is the Subjunctive?*, p. 78). This mood is not divided into tenses.

> They suggested that he *do* it right away.
> I wish that Anita *were* with me.

IN ITALIAN

The Italian language identifies four moods: the indicative, the imperative, the subjunctive, and the conditional.

Indicative — As in English, the indicative mood is the most common, and most of the tenses you will learn belong to this mood.

Imperative — As in English, the imperative mood is used to give commands and it is not divided into tenses.

40

Subjunctive — Unlike English, the subjunctive mood is used very frequently and it is divided into tenses: present, past, imperfect, and past perfect.

Conditional — Italian grammar also recognizes a mood called the conditional. The conditional mood is used to express the possibility of a result if a certain condition is fulfilled and also to express polite requests. (See *What is the Conditional?*, p. 81.)

17

WHAT IS MEANT BY TENSE?

The TENSE of a verb indicates the time when the action of the verb takes place: at the present time, in the past, or in the future.

I am studying	PRESENT
I studied	PAST
I will study	FUTURE

As you can see in the above examples, just by putting the verb in a different tense, and without giving any additional information such as "I am studying *now,*" "I studied *yesterday,*" or "I will study *tomorrow,*" you can indicate when the action of the verb takes place.

Tenses may be classified according to the way they are formed. A SIMPLE TENSE consists of only one verb form *(studied)*, while a COMPOUND TENSE consists of two or more verb forms *(am studying)*.

Since the indicative mood is the mood most frequently used, we will consider only tenses of the indicative in this section (see *What is Meant by Mood?*, p. 47). The tenses of the other moods will be treated in separate chapters (see *What is the Subjunctive?*, p. 78 and *What is the Conditional?*, p. 81).

IN ENGLISH

Listed below are the main tenses whose equivalents you will encounter in Italian.

PRESENT

I study	PRESENT
I am studying	PRESENT PROGRESSIVE

PAST

I studied	SIMPLE PAST
I have studied	PRESENT PERFECT
I was studying	PAST PROGRESSIVE
I had studied	PAST PERFECT

FUTURE

I will study	FUTURE
I will have studied	FUTURE PERFECT

As you can see, there are only two simple tenses, the present and the simple past. All of the other tenses are compound tenses formed by one or more auxiliary verbs plus the main verb (see *What is an Auxiliary Verb?*, p. 26).

IN ITALIAN

Listed below are the tenses of the indicative mood that you will encounter in Italian.

studio	*I study* *I am studying* *I do study*	PRESENT **PRESENTE**
studiai	*I studied*	SIMPLE PAST **PASSATO REMOTO**[1]
ho studiato	*I studied* *I have studied*	PRESENT PERFECT **PASSATO PROSSIMO**
studiavo	*I studied* *I used to study* *I was studying*	IMPERFECT **IMPERFETTO**
avevo studiato	*I had studied*	PAST PERFECT **TRAPASSATO PROSSIMO**
studierò	*I will study*	FUTURE **FUTURO**
avrò studiato	*I will have studied*	FUTURE PERFECT **FUTURO ANTERIORE**

As you can see, there are more simple tenses in Italian than in English: present, simple past, imperfect, and future. The others are compound tenses which are formed with either the auxiliary verb **avere** *to have* or the auxiliary verb **essere** *to be* + the past participle of the main verb (see pp. 60-1 in *What is a Participle?*).

This handbook discusses the formation of the various tenses and their usage in separate sections: *What is the Present Tense?*, p. 51; *What is a Past Tense?*, p. 62; *What is the Past Perfect Tense?*, p. 68; *What is the Future Tense?*, p. 70; *What is the Future Perfect Tense?*, p. 73.

CAREFUL — There is often a lack of correspondence between verb tenses in English and Italian. For example, the English present progressive form "I *am studying*" usually corresponds to the Italian simple present tense **studio**. Make sure that you are using the tense appropriate for that language.

[1]This tense is used primarily in literary and historical texts, not in modern spoken Italian. The present perfect (**passato prossimo**) is the usual Italian equivalent of the simple past in English.

WHAT IS THE PRESENT TENSE?

The PRESENT TENSE indicates that the action is taking place at   1
the present time. It can be:

- when the speaker is speaking   I *see* you.
- a habitual action   He *smokes* all the time.
- a general truth   The sun *rises* every day.

IN ENGLISH

There are three forms of the verb which, although they
have slightly different meanings, indicate the present
tense.

Mary *studies* in the library.   PRESENT
Mary *is studying* in the library.   PRESENT PROGRESSIVE   10
Mary *does study* in the library.   PRESENT EMPHATIC

When you answer the following questions, you will auto-
matically choose one of the above forms.

Where does Mary study?
Mary *studies* in the library.

Where is Mary studying?
Mary *is studying* in the library.

Does Mary usually study in the library?
Yes, Mary usually *does study* in the library, not in her room.   20

IN ITALIAN

The present tense can be used to express the meaning of
the English present, present progressive, and present
emphatic tenses. In Italian the idea of the present tense is
indicated by the ending of the verb (see p. 39).

*Mary **studies** in the library.*

present → **studia**

*Mary **is studying** in the library.*

present progressive → **studia**   30

*Mary **does study** in the library.*

present emphatic → **studia**

CAREFUL — There is a present progressive tense in Italian,
but since it is not used in the same manner as the English
present progressive, we have discussed it in a separate section. (See *What are the Progressive Tenses?*, p. 55.)

WHAT ARE SOME EQUIVALENTS OF "TO BE"?

The verb *to be* can be used as an auxiliary verb or as a main verb. In this chapter we will limit ourselves to its use as a main verb (see *What is an Auxiliary Verb?*, p. 26).

IN ENGLISH

The verb *to be* (whose forms are often contracted to *'m, 's, 're*) is used in a variety of ways:

- for indicating the existence of someone or something; who or what *there is* or *there are* in a given place

    There is only one boy in our class. [There*'s* only...]
    There are many drugstores downtown.

- for pointing out the location of someone or something

    There *is* my friend, over there. [There*'s*...]
    There *are* my books, on the coffee table.

- for telling time

    It *is* 4:00. [It*'s* ..]

- for discussing health

    John *isn't* very well.

- for indicating weather conditions

    It *is* cold today. [It*'s* ..]

- for describing traits and characteristics

    You *are* very tall. [You*'re*...]

- for expressing physical sensations or feelings

    I *am* hungry. [I*'m*...]
    She *is* happy. [She*'s*...]

- for telling age

    I *am* twenty years old. [I*'m*...]

IN ITALIAN

In most cases the verb **essere** and the English verb *to be* correspond. However, there are many idiomatic expressions which require the use of another verb or expression.

ENGLISH	ITALIAN
to be	**avere** *to have*
	fare *to make, to do*
	stare *to stay*
there is, there are	**c'è, ci sono** or **ecco**

Here are a few rules to help you select the appropriate Italian verb.

To be → **avere**
There are some common idiomatic constructions which use the verb *to be* in English and the verb *to have* **avere** in Italian. These expressions will have to be memorized. Here are a few examples.

- for expressing many physical sensations or feelings

  I am hungry.
  to be

  Ho fame.
  to have [lit. I have hunger]

- for telling age

  I am twenty years old.
  to be

  Ho vent'anni.
  to have [lit. I have twenty years]

To be → **fare**
English uses the verb *to be* to indicate weather conditions, and Italian uses the verb **fare** *to make, to do.*

  It is cold today.
  to be

  Fa freddo oggi.
  to make [lit. it makes cold today]

To be → **stare**
English uses the verb *to be* to discuss health, while Italian uses the verb **stare** *to stay.*

  John is not very well.
  to be

  Giovanni non **sta** molto bene.
  to stay [lit. John isn't staying very well]

There is, there are → **c'è, ci sono,** or **ecco**
The English expressions *there is* and *there are* are translated in two different ways depending on their meaning.

- to indicate the existence of someone or something →
  c'è *there is,* **ci sono** *there are*

40

50

60

70

There is only one boy in our class.
C'è soltanto un ragazzo nella nostra classe.

There are many drugstores downtown.
Ci sono molte farmacie in centro.

- to emphasize the location of something or someone →
  ecco *there is* or *there are*

  There is my friend.
  Ecco il mio amico.

  There are my books.
  Ecco i miei libri.

Notice that **ecco** is invariable (it does not change) and that it is not followed by a verb.

CAREFUL — Do not confuse **c'è**, **ci sono** *to indicate existence* with **ecco** *to point out location.*

There is a new Italian professor. [at our school]
C'è un nuovo professore d'italiano.

There is the new Italian professor. [pointing to him]
Ecco il nuovo professore d'italiano.

WHAT ARE THE PROGRESSIVE TENSES?

The **PROGRESSIVE TENSES** are used to emphasize that actions are   1
in progress at a specific moment in time.

> John *is talking* on the phone. [right now]
> We *were trying* to start the car. [at a time in the past]

IN ENGLISH

The progressive tenses are made up of the auxiliary verb *to be* + the present participle of the main verb (see *What is an Auxiliary Verb?*, p. 26 and *What is a Participle?*, p. 57).

> We *are **leaving*** right now.
>
> | present participle of main verb *to leave*
> present tense of *to be*   10

> At that moment John *was **washing*** his car.
>
> | present participle
> | main verb *to wash*
> past tense of *to be*

Notice that it is the tense of the auxiliary verb *to be* that indicates when the action of the main verb takes place.

IN ITALIAN

The progressive tenses are made up of the auxiliary verb **stare** *to be* conjugated in the various tenses + the GERUNDIO[1]   20
of the main verb. The **gerundio** is formed by adding -**ando** to the stem of -**are** verbs and -**endo** to the stem of -**ere** and -**ire** verbs.

INFINITIVE	STEM	GERUNDIO
cant**are**	cant-	cant**ando**
tem**ere**	tem-	tem**endo**
part**ire**	part-	part**endo**

Here we shall be concerned only with the present progressive which is made up of the present tense of **stare** + the **gerundio** of the main verb.   30

> *Stiamo uscendo* in questo stesso momento.
>
> present   "gerundio"
> **stare**   **uscire**
> *to be*   *to go out*
> ***We are going out*** *right now.*

---

[1]Do not confuse the term **gerundio** which is an Italian verb form with *gerund* which is a verbal noun in English (see p. 59).

Stai studiando ora?

present   "gerundio"
stare   **studiare**
to be   *to study*
*Are you **studying** right now?*

PRESENT VS. PRESENT PROGRESSIVE TENSE
IN ENGLISH

The present progressive tense is used to describe habitual actions, to state general truths, and to describe an action that is taking place at a specific moment. It is used far more frequently in English than in Italian.

IN ITALIAN

The present progressive tense is used only to emphasize an action that is taking place at a particular moment or to stress the continuity of an action. The present tense, and not the present progressive tense, is used to describe habitual action or to state general truths (see *What is the Present Tense?*, p. 51).

Compare the use of the present tense and present progressive tense in the sentences below.

*John, what **are** you **studying** in school?*

present tense → **studi**
The present tense is used in Italian because you are asking what John is studying in general over a period of time.

*John, what **are** you **studying** now?*

present progressive → **stai studiando**
The present progressive is used in Italian because the word *now* indicates that you want to know what John is studying at this particular time as opposed to all other times.

*Mary, **are** you **working** for the government?*

present tense → **lavori**
The present tense is used in Italian because you are asking where Mary is working in general over a period of time.

*Mary, **are** you **working** these days?*

present progressive → **stai lavorando**
The present progressive is used in Italian because the words *these days* indicate that you want to know if Mary is working at this particular time as opposed to all other times.

CAREFUL — Do not use the present progressive to state general truths or habitual actions; use the present tense instead.

WHAT IS A PARTICIPLE?

A PARTICIPLE is a form of a verb which can be used in one of
two ways: with an auxiliary verb to form certain tenses or as
an adjective to modify or describe a noun (see *What is an Auxiliary Verb?*, p. 26).

I was *writing* a letter.

auxiliary participle
past progressive tense

The *broken* vase was on the floor.

participle describing *vase*

Participles are found in two tenses: the present participle and
the past participle. As you will learn, participles are not
always used in the same way in English and Italian.

PRESENT PARTICIPLE
IN ENGLISH

The present participle is easy to recognize because it is an
-ing form of the verb: *working, studying, dancing, playing.*

The present participle has two primary uses:

1. as an adjective

This is an *amazing* discovery.

describes the noun *discovery*

2. in verbal functions

▪ as the main verb in compound tenses with the auxiliary
verb *to be* (see *What are the Progressive Tenses?*, p. 55)

She is *singing.*

present progressive of *to sing*

They were *dancing.*

past progressive of *to dance*

▪ in a participial phrase

(By) *studying* hard, Carl learned Italian.

participial phrase

IN ITALIAN

The present participle is formed by adding **-ante** to the stem of **-are** verbs and **-ente** to the stem of **-ere** and **-ire** verbs.

INFINITIVE	STEM	PRESENT PARTICIPLE
interess**are**	interess-	interess**ante**
sorprend**ere**	sorprend-	sorprend**ente**
segu**ire**	segu-	segu**ente**

The present participle is used mainly as an adjective, in the same way as English.

> Questa è una scoperta **sorprendente**.
> *This is an an **amazing** discovery.*

"GERUNDIO"

The two verbal functions (progressive tenses and participial phrases) of the English present participle are expressed in Italian by the **gerundio**. (Do not confuse **gerundio** which is an Italian verb form with the term *gerund* which is an English verbal noun, see p. 59.)

1. The progressive tenses are made up of the auxiliary verb **stare** + the **gerundio** of the main verb. (See *What are the Progressive Tenses?*, p. 55 for a detailed study.)

present progressive
*She is **singing**.*

present participle
Sta **cantando**.

present	"gerundio"
stare	**cantare**
to be	*to sing*

past progressive
*They were **dancing**.*

present participle
Stavano **ballando**.

imperfect	"gerundio"
stare	**ballare**
to be	*to sing*

2. The participial phrase is expressed with the **gerundio** alone; the preposition which is optional in English is not used in Italian.

participial phrase
⌐‾‾‾‾‾‾‾⌐
*(By) **studying** hard, Carl learned Italian.*

present participle
Studiando sodo, Carlo ha imparato l'italiano.   80

"gerundio"

GERUND

An English verb form ending in *-ing* is not always a present participle; it can be a verbal noun. A **VERBAL NOUN**, also called a **GERUND**, is a verb form which functions like a noun.

IN ENGLISH

The verbal noun ends in *-ing* and can function in almost any way a noun can. It can be the subject, direct object, indirect object and an object of a preposition.   90

Reading can be fun.

noun subject

Mario prefers *reading*.

noun direct object

Before *leaving*, call me.

noun object of preposition

IN ITALIAN

The English gerund is expressed with the infinitive of the   100
Italian verb.

***Reading** is fun.*

gerund
Leggere è divertente.

infinitive

*Mario prefers **reading**.*

gerund
Mario preferisce **leggere**.   110

infinitive

*Before **leaving**, call me.*

gerund
Prima di **partire**, telefonami.

infinitive

SUMMARY

For reference, here is a chart identifying the various English *-ing* forms and their Italian equivalents.

ENGLISH "-ING"		ITALIAN
	ADJECTIVE	
PRESENT PARTICIPLE ⟶		PRESENT PARTICIPLE
the *reading* public		$\begin{cases} \text{-are} \rightarrow \textbf{-ante} \\ \text{-ere/-ire} \rightarrow \textbf{-ente} \end{cases}$
	VERB	
PROGRESSIVE TENSES		
■ *to be* + **present participle** ⟶		VARIOUS SIMPLE TENSES
What *are* you *reading?*		present
What *were* you *reading?*		imperfect
etc.		etc.
■ *to be* + **present participle** ⟶		STARE + "GERUNDIO"
What *are* you *reading* now?		$\begin{cases} \text{-are} \rightarrow \textbf{-ando} \\ \text{-ere, -ire} \rightarrow \textbf{-endo} \end{cases}$
PARTICIPIAL PHRASE ⟶		"GERUNDIO"
(while) *reading*		
	NOUN	
GERUND ⟶		INFINITIVE
Reading is fun.		**-are, -ere, -ire**
Without *reading,* life is boring.		

PAST PARTICIPLE

IN ENGLISH

The past participle is formed in several ways. You can always identify it by remembering the form of the verb that follows *I have: I have spoken, I have written, I have walked.*

The past participle has two primary uses:

1. as an adjective

> Is the *written* word more important than the *spoken* word?
>
> describes the noun *word*   describes the noun *word*

2. as the main verb in compound tenses with the auxiliary verb *to have*

> I *have written* all that I have to say.
> He *hadn't spoken* to me since our quarrel.

IN ITALIAN

Most verbs have a regular past participle formed according to the regular pattern: **-are** verbs add **-ato** to the stem, **-ere** verbs add **-uto**, and **-ire** verbs add **-ito**.

Infinitive	Stem	Past participle	
cantare	cant-	cantato	160
temere	tem-	temuto	
partire	part-	partito	

You will have to memorize irregular past participles individually.

As in English the past participle can be used as part of a compound verb or as an adjective.

1. The most important use of the past participle in Italian is as a verb form in combination with the auxiliary verb **avere** *to have:* **ho cantato** *I have sung* or **essere** *to be:* 170 **sono partita** *I have left* to form the perfect tenses (see *What is Meant by Tense?*, p. 49).

2. as an adjective

   When the past participle is used as an adjective, it must agree with the noun it modifies in gender and number.

   *the **spoken** language*

   > *Spoken* modifies the noun *language*. Since **la lingua** *language* is feminine singular, the word for *spoken* must be feminine singular.

   la lingua **parlata** 180

   *the **broken** records*

   > *Broken* modifies the noun *records*. Since **i dischi** *records* is masculine plural, the word for *broken* must be masculine plural.

   i dischi **rotti**

WHAT IS A PAST TENSE?

A PAST TENSE is used to express an action or circumstances of an action in the past.

IN ENGLISH

There are several verb forms that can be used to refer to the past.

I worked	SIMPLE PAST
I did work	PAST EMPHATIC
I have worked	PRESENT PERFECT
I was working	PAST PROGRESSIVE
I had worked	PAST PERFECT

Simple past — The simple past is called "simple" because it is a simple tense, i.e., it consists of one word *(worked* in the example above). Regular verbs add **-ed** to the dictionary form to form the simple past: *played, worked.* Irregular verbs are unpredictable; they can be spelled differently: to speak → *spoke*; or they can be pronounced differently *to read* → *read.*

The other past tenses are compound tenses; i.e., they consist of more than one word.

Past emphatic — The past emphatic is composed of the auxiliary verb *to do* in the past tense *(did)* + the dictionary form of the main verb: *I did work, he did play.*

Present perfect — The present perfect is composed of the auxiliary verb *to have* in the present tense + the past participle of the main verb: *I have worked, he has played.* (See *What is an Auxiliary Verb?*, p. 26 and *What is a Participle?*, p. 57.

Past progressive — The past progressive is composed of the auxiliary verb *to be* in the past tense + the present participle of the main verb : *I was working, he was playing.* (See *What are the Progressive Tenses?*, p. 55.)

Past perfect — The past perfect is composed of the auxiliary verb *to have* in the past tense + the past participle of the main verb: *I had worked, he had played.* (See *What is the Past Perfect Tense?*, p. 68.)

IN ITALIAN

There are several verb tenses that can be used to refer to the past. Each tense has its own set of endings and its own rules as to when and how to use it. We will here be concerned with the two most frequently used past tenses in Italian: the present perfect and the imperfect.

Present perfect (passato prossimo)

The present perfect, called **passato prossimo**, is composed of the present tense of the auxiliary verbs **avere** *to have* or **essere** *to be* + the past participle of the main verb. It usually corresponds to the English simple past; sometimes the present perfect or the past emphatic is more appropriate.

Ho giocato nel parco.
auxiliary main
avere   verb
present   past participle
 └─ passato prossimo ─┘
I played in the park.
simple past
I have played in the park.
 └─ present perfect ─┘
I did play in the park.
 └─ past emphatic ─┘

Sono andato al parco.
auxiliary main
essere   verb
present   past participle
 └─ passato prossimo ─┘
I went to the park.
simple past
I have gone to the park.
 └─ present perfect ─┘
I did go to the park.
 └─ past emphatic ─┘

Selection of the auxiliary avere or essere

Unlike English where the present perfect tense is always formed with the auxiliary verb *to have*, in Italian the **passato prossimo** can be formed with either **avere** or **essere**. Therefore, you will need to know how to determine which auxiliary is required.

40

50

60

70

80

Here are some guidelines to help you select the correct auxiliary.

1. All transitive verbs (the verbs which can take a direct object, see p. 118) use the auxiliary **avere**.
2. All reflexive verbs use the auxiliary **essere** (see *What is a Reflexive Verb?*, p. 86).
3. Intransitive verbs (the verbs which do not take a direct object, see p. 118) can use **avere** or **essere** as an auxiliary. Since most intransitive verbs take **avere** as an auxiliary, it is simpler to memorize the relatively short list of verbs which take **essere** and assume the others use **avere**.

Here is a basic list of commonly used "**essere** verbs." The first eight verbs have been grouped together because they can easily be memorized by associating them in pairs of opposites:

andare	*to go*	≠	venire	*to come*
arrivare	*to arrive*	≠	partire	*to leave*
entrare	*to enter*	≠	uscire	*to go out*
morire	*to die*	≠	nascere	*to be born*
essere	*to be*		parere	*to seem*
avvenire	*to happen*		piacere	*to like*
dipendere	*to depend*		restare	*to stay*
dispiacere	*to be sorry*		riuscire	*to succeed*
diventare	*to become*		stare	*to stay, to feel*

A more complete list of the intransitive verbs which take **essere** can be found in the Appendix of your Italian textbook. When you are in doubt about which auxiliary to use, consult an Italian dictionary under the verb infinitive.

Agreement of the past participle

The past participle follows different rules of agreement depending on whether the auxiliary verb used is **essere** or **avere**.

1. When the auxiliary verb is **essere**, the past participle agrees in gender and number with the subject of the verb (see *What is a Subject?*, p. 28).

> **Paola** è **arrivata** dall' Italia.
> subject   past participle
>   └ fem. sing. ┘
> ***Paula arrived*** *from Italy.*

Mario è **arrivato** dall' Italia.

subject   past participle
└ masc. sing. ┘

Mario arrived from Italy.

Paola e **sua sorella** sono **arrivate** dall' Italia.

subjects   past participle
└ fem. pl. ┘

Paula and her sister arrived from Italy.

2. When the auxiliary verb is **avere**, the past participle agrees in gender and number with the direct object pronoun when it precedes the verb in the sentence (see p. 124 in *What is an Object Pronoun?*). If the direct object comes after the verb, there is no agreement and the past participle remains in the masculine singular form; i.e., the form that is found in the dictionary.

Quando hai visto Carla? **L**'ho **vista** ieri.

direct object   past participle
refers to *Carla*
└ fem. sing. ┘

en did you see Carla? I **saw her** yesterday.

ando hai visto Franco? **L**'ho **visto** ieri.

direct object   past participle
refers to *Franco*
└ masc. sing. ┘

en did you see Frank? I **saw him** yesterday.

ando hai visto Franco e suo fratello? **Li** ho **visti** ieri.

direct object past participle
refers to *Franco e suo fratello*
└ masc. pl. ┘

When did you see Frank and his brother? I **saw them** *yesterday.*

Your textbook will go over this rule in detail.

Imperfect (imperfetto)

The imperfect, called the **imperfetto**, is a simple tense formed with the stem of the verb (see p. 24) + a regular set of endings: (io) parl**avo**, (tu) legg**evi**, (lui) fin**iva**, etc. Your textbook will provide all of the forms and irregularities.

There are two English verb forms that indicate that the imperfect should be used in Italian:

1. when the English verb form includes, or could include, the expression *used to*

*I **played** soccer every afternoon.*

> *I played* could be replaced by *I used to play*; therefore, the Italian equivalent is the imperfect.

Giocavo a calcio ogni pomeriggio.

2. when the English verb form is in the past progressive, as in *was playing, was studying*

*I **was playing** soccer in the park.*

Giocavo a calcio nel parco.

In addition, verbs describing physical, mental, and emotional states, as well as age, weather, and time of day in the past are usually put in the **imperfetto**.

*I **was** very tired, but I **was** happy.*

Ero molto stanca, ma **ero** felice.

*It **was** four o'clock.*

Erano le quattro.

Except for the two verb forms listed under 1. and 2. above, the English verb tense will not indicate to you whether you should use the **passato prossimo** or the **imperfetto**.

Selecting the passato prossimo or the imperfetto

Both the **passato prossimo** and the **imperfetto** refer to events which occurred in the past. You will have to learn to analyze sentences and their context so that you can decide which of the two tenses is appropriate. As a general guideline, remember the following:

PASSATO PROSSIMO	▪ tells "what happened" a specific, completed action
IMPERFETTO	▪ tells "what one used to do" a habitual or repeated action
	▪ tells "what was going on" an action in progress
	▪ tells "what things were like" a description

Consider the sentence "I *played* in the park." In English, the same form of the verb (*played*) is used; however, in Italian the tense of the verb **giocare** *to play* will be different depending on the question being answered.

▪ "What happened?"

*Where **did you play** yesterday? **I played** in the park.*

> The question: "what happened" at a specific time, i.e., yesterday; therefore the Italian equivalents of the verbs will be in the **passato prossimo**.

Dove **hai giocato** ieri? **Ho giocato** nel parco.

    passato prossimo   passato prossimo

- "What did you used to do?"

  *Where **did you play** when you were a child? I **played** in the park.*
  The question: "what did you used to do;" therefore the
  Italian equivalents of the verbs will be in the **imperfetto**.
  Dove **giocavi** da bambino? **Giocavo** nel parco.   210

  imperfetto   imperfetto

- "What was going on?"

  Since the **passato prossimo** and the **imperfetto** can
  indicate actions that took place during the same time
  period in the past, you will often find the two tenses
  intermingled in a sentence or a story.

  *He **was reading** when I **arrived**.*
  Both actions "reading" and "arrived" took place at the same
  time in the past.
  What was going on? He was reading → **imperfetto**   220
  What happened? I arrived → **passato prossimo**
  Leggeva quando **sono arrivato**.

  imperfetto   passato prossimo

Your Italian textbook will give you additional guidelines
to help you to select the appropriate past tense. You can
practice by analyzing paragraphs written in the past tense
in English and indicating whether the **passato prossimo**
or the **imperfetto** would be used in Italian. Sometimes
either tense is possible grammatically, but usually one of
the two is more logical or appropriate.   230

CHAPTER

23

WHAT IS THE PAST PERFECT TENSE?

The PAST PERFECT tense is used to express an action completed in the past before some other past action or event.

IN ENGLISH

The past perfect is formed with the auxiliary verb *to have* in the past tense *(had)* + the past participle of the main verb.

The past perfect is used when two actions happened at different times in the past and you want to make it clear which of the actions preceded the other.

She suddenly *remembered* that she *had* not *eaten* yet.

             past tense   past perfect
                1   2

Both action 1 and action 2 occurred in the past, but action 2 preceded action 1. Therefore, action 2 is in the past perfect.

The tense of a verb indicates the time when an action occurs. Therefore, when two verbs in a sentence are in the same tense, we know that the actions took place at the same time. In order to indicate that they took place at different times, different tenses must be used. Look at the following examples:

The car *was sliding* because it *was raining*.

      past progressive   past progressive
           1   2

Action 1 and action 2 were taking place at the same time.

The car *was sliding* because it *had rained*.

      past progressive   past perfect
           1   2

Action 2 took place before action 1.

IN ITALIAN

The past perfect, called **trapassato prossimo**, is formed with the auxiliary verb **avere** *to have* or **essere** *to be* in the imperfect tense + the past participle of the main verb. The rules for the selection of the appropriate auxiliary and for the agreement of the past participle are the same as for the present perfect (see pp. 64-5).

The past perfect is used to indicate that an action in the past took place before another action in the past, expressed by the present perfect or the imperfect.

Look at this line showing the relationship of tenses. 40

VERB TENSE:	PAST PERFECT	PAST	PRESENT
	Trapassato prossimo	Passato prossimo Imperfetto	Present
	- 2	- 1	0
	x	x	x

TIME ACTION TAKES PLACE:	0 now
	- 1 before 0
	- 2 before -1

Same verb tense → same moment in time 50

*The car **was sliding** because it **was raining**.*
La macchina **sbandava** perchè **pioveva**.

     imperfect   imperfect
       -1   -1

When both verbs are in the imperfect the two actions were taking place at the same time in the past.

Different verb tense → different moments in time

*The car **was sliding** because it **had rained**.*
La macchina **sbandava** perchè **aveva piovuto**.

     imperfect   past perfect   60
       -1   -2

The action in the past perfect -2 occurred before the action in the imperfect -1.

CAREFUL — You cannot always rely on English to determine when to use the past perfect. If it is clear which action came first, English usage permits the use of the simple past to describe an action that preceded another.

*The teacher **wanted** to know who **saw** the student.*

     simple past   simple past
                                 70
*The teacher **wanted** to know who **had seen** the student.*

     simple past   past perfect

In Italian, only the verb sequence of the sentence with the past perfect would be correct.

Il professore **voleva** sapere chi **aveva veduto** lo studente.

     imperfetto   trapassato prossimo
       -1   -2

The verb in the past perfect "had seen" (-2) stresses that the action was completed before the action of "wanted to know"(-1).

CHAPTER

24

WHAT IS THE FUTURE TENSE?

1   The **FUTURE TENSE** indicates that an action will take place in
the future.

> We'll *meet* you tomorrow.

IN ENGLISH

The future tense is a compound tense. It is formed with
the auxiliary *will* or *shall* + the main verb. Note that *shall*
is used only in the first person singular and plural and
only in formal English and British English. *Will* occurs in
everyday language.

10

> Paul and Mary *will do* their work tomorrow.
> I *shall* go out tonight.

In conversation, *shall* and *will* are often shortened to *'ll* :
"They*'ll do* it tomorrow," "I*'ll go* out tonight."

IN ITALIAN

You do not need an auxiliary verb to show that the action
will take place in the future. The future tense, called
futuro, is indicated by a simple tense. It is formed with a
stem derived from the infinitive + future tense endings.

- **-are** verbs → drop the final -e + change **-ar-** to **-er-** +

20   future endings

INFINITIVE	STEM +	FUTURE ENDING	
parl**are**	parler-	parlerò	*I shall//will speak*
cant**are**	canter-	canterà	*she will sing*

- **-ere** and **-ire** verbs → drop the final **-e** + future endings

INFINITIVE	STEM +	FUTURE ENDING	
tem**ere**	temer-	temerò	*I shall//will fear*
part**ire**	partir-	partirà	*he will leave*

30   - irregular verbs have irregular future stems + future endings

INFINITIVE	STEM +	FUTURE ENDING	
andare	andr-	andrò	*I shall//will go*
avere	avr-	avrà	*she will have*

Your textbook will indicate which verbs have irregular
stems in the future. The same stem serves to form the conditional (see *What is the Conditional?*, p. 81).

SUBSTITUTE FOR THE FUTURE TENSE
In English and in Italian it is possible to express a future action without using the future tense.

IN ENGLISH
There are two possible substitutes for the future tense.

- the present progressive of the main verb (see *What are the Progressive Tenses?*, p. 55)

    We *are leaving* tonight.
    present progressive *to leave*

- the present progressive of *to go* + the infinitive of the main verb

    We *are going to leave* tonight.
    present infinitive
    progressive
    to go

Both of these constructions have the same meaning as the future tense: "We *shall leave* tonight."

IN ITALIAN
The above progressive constructions are not used. In the spoken language the present tense commonly replaces the future tense to indicate an action about to take place.

Partiamo stasera.
present
We **will leave** *tonight*.
future

Elena **resta** a casa stasera.
present
Helen **will stay** *home tonight*.
future

CAREFUL — While English uses the present tense after expressions such as *as soon as, when,* and *by the time,* which introduce an action that will take place in the future, Italian uses the future tense.

As soon as he **returns**, *I* **will call** *him*.
present future
Appena **ritornerà**, gli **telefonerò**.
future future

FUTURE OF PROBABILITY

80 When the speaker expresses a probable fact, it is called the
FUTURE OF PROBABILITY.

IN ENGLISH

The idea of probability is expressed with words such as
must, probably, wonder.

> I *wonder* who is at the door.
> It is *probably* my mother.
> Charles *must* have it.

IN ITALIAN

90 The future tense can be used to express a probable fact,
without the use of words such as *must, probably, wonder.*

> *I **wonder** who **is** at the door. It **is probably** my mother.*
> | |
>   present tense   present tense
> Chi **sarà** alla porta? **Sarà** mia madre.
> | |
>   future tense   future tense

> *I can't find my book. Charles **must have** it.*
> |
>   present tense
> Non posso trovare il mio libro. L'**avrà** Carlo.
> |
>   future tense

WHAT IS THE FUTURE PERFECT TENSE?

The FUTURE PERFECT TENSE is used to express an action which will be completed in the future before some other future action or by a specific time.

I *will have finished* my degree by next spring.

IN ENGLISH

The future perfect is formed with the auxiliaries *will have* or *shall have* + past participle of the main verb: *I shall have taken, he will have gone.* Note that *shall* is used only in formal English and British English.

They will have left before he arrives.

future perfect   future action
1   2

Although the verb of action 2 is in the present tense, it refers to a future action. Action 1 is in the future perfect as it will be completed in the future before action 2 takes place.

They will have left by 10:00 P.M.

future perfect   specific time in the future
1   2

Action 1 is in the future perfect because it will be completed in the future before a specific time in the future (2).

Observe the sequence of events expressed by the future tenses in the following time-line.

VERB TENSE:	Present	Future Perfect	Future action specific time in the future
	0	1	2
	x	x	x

TIME ACTION TAKES PLACE: 0 → now
1 → after 0 and before 2
2 → after 1

To use the future perfect (point 1) you have to have an action or event at point 2 with which to relate it.

IN ITALIAN

The future perfect, called the **futuro anteriore**, is formed with the auxiliary **avere** *to have* or **essere** *to be* in the future tense + the past participle of the main verb: **avrò preso** *I will have taken*, **sarà partito** *he will have gone*.

English and Italian coincide in the use of the future perfect to refer to an action which will have been completed by a future time.

Saranno partiti prima che lui arrivi.

       future perfect   future action
            1   2

They will have left before he arrives.

Although the verb of action 2 is in the present subjunctive (in English, it is in the present tense), it refers to a future action. In both English and Italian action 1 is in the future perfect, as it will be completed in the future before action 2.

Saranno partiti entro le dieci.

       future perfect   specific time in the future
            1   2

They will have left by ten o'clock.

Future Perfect in Dependent Clauses

The most frequent use of the future perfect in Italian, however, is in a dependent clause introduced by a time conjunction such as **dopo che**, **appena**, **quando**, etc. This clause refers to an action in the future to be completed before the main action (1), which is expressed in the future tense. Here Italian always requires the use of the future perfect (2), whereas English uses the present perfect (2).

Stasera **usciremo** dopo che i bambini **avranno mangiato**

          future (1)   future perfect (2)

e **saranno andati** a letto.

    future perfect (2)

*This evening, we **will go out** after the children **have eaten***

               future (1)   present perfect (2)

*and **gone** to bed.*

   present perfect (2)

WHAT IS THE IMPERATIVE?

The IMPERATIVE is the verb form to give a command or to make a suggestion. There are affirmative imperatives (to tell someone to do something) and negative imperatives (to tell someone not to do something).

AFFIRMATIVE IMPERATIVE	*Open* the door!
NEGATIVE IMPERATIVE	*Don't open* the door!

IN ENGLISH

There are two forms of commands, depending on who is being told to do, or not to do, something.

"You" command — When addressing one or more persons the dictionary form of the verb is used.

AFFIRMATIVE IMPERATIVE	NEGATIVE IMPERATIVE
Answer the phone.	*Don't answer* the phone.
Clean your room.	*Don't clean* your room.

Notice that the subject pronoun "you" is not used. The absence of the pronoun *you* in the sentence indicates that the verb form is an imperative and not a present tense.

You answer the phone.	PRESENT TENSE
Answer the phone.	AFFIRMATIVE IMPERATIVE
Don't answer the phone.	NEGATIVE IMPERATIVE

"We" command — When the speaker makes a suggestion that includes himself and others, the phrase "let's" (a contraction of "let us") + the dictionary form of the verb is used.

AFFIRMATIVE IMPERATIVE	NEGATIVE IMPERATIVE
Let's leave.	*Let's not leave.*
Let's go to the movies.	*Let's not go* to the movies.

IN ITALIAN

As in English, there are affirmative and negative commands.

"You" command — There are many forms of the *you* command to distinguish familiar and formal as well as affirmative and negative commands (see pp. 32-4 in *What is a Subject Pronoun?*).

Here are examples of each form.

■ an order given to someone you address in the familiar form, i.e., someone to whom you say **tu**

The affirmative imperative form is based on the present indicative: **-are** verbs have the same form as the 3rd person singular and **-ere** and **-ire** verbs have the same form as the 2nd person singular. The negative imperative form is the same as the verb's infinitive.

AFFIRMATIVE	NEGATIVE
Parla!	Non parlare!
Speak!	*Don't speak!*
Scrivi!	Non scrivere!
Write!	*Don't write!*
Parti!	Non partire!
Leave!	*Don't leave!*

■ an order given to two or more persons you address in the familiar form, i.e., to whom you would say **tu** individually

The affirmative and the negative imperatives have the same form as the 2nd person plural of the present indicative.

AFFIRMATIVE	NEGATIVE
Parlate!	Non parlate!
Speak!	*Don't speak!*
Scrivete!	Non scrivete!
Write!	*Don't write!*
Partite!	Non partite!
Leave!	*Don't leave!*

■ an order given to a person you address in the formal form, i.e., to whom you say **Lei**

The affirmative and negative imperatives have the same form as the 3rd person singular of the present subjunctive (see *What is the Subjunctive?*, p. 78).

AFFIRMATIVE	NEGATIVE
Parli!	Non parli!
Speak!	*Don't speak!*
Scriva!	Non scriva!
Write!	*Don't write!*
Parta!	Non parta!
Leave!	*Don't leave!*

■ when an order is given to two or more persons you address in the formal form, i.e., to whom you would say **Lei** individually.

The affirmative and negative imperatives have the same form as the 3rd person plural of the present subjunctive.

AFFIRMATIVE	NEGATIVE
Parlino!	Non parlino!
Speak!	*Don't speak!*
Scrivano!	Non scrivano!
Write!	*Don't write!*
Partano!	Non partano!
Leave!	*Don't leave!*

"We" command — This form is used to give commands or advice to oneself plus others.

The affirmative and negative imperatives have the same form as the 1st person plural of the present indicative.

AFFIRMATIVE	NEGATIVE
Parliamo!	Non parliamo!
Let's speak!	*Let's **not** speak!*
Scriviamo!	Non scriviamo!
Let's write!	*Let's **not** write!*
Partiamo!	Non partiamo!
Let's leave!	*Let's **not** leave!*

SUMMARY

For reference, here is a chart showing the affirmative and negative Italian command forms. Note that all of the imperative forms, except the **tu** forms, are the same in the affirmative and negative.

	AFFIRMATIVE		NEGATIVE
tu	PRESENT INDICATIVE		INFINITIVE
	-are: 3rd pers. sing.		
		parla	non parlare
	-ere, -ire: 2nd pers. sing.		
		scrivi	non scrivere
		parti	non partire
voi		PRESENT INDICATIVE	
	2nd pers. pl.		
		parlate	non parlate
Lei		PRESENT SUBJUNCTIVE	
	3rd pers. sing.		
		parli	non parli
Loro		PRESENT SUBJUNCTIVE	
	3rd pers. pl.		
		parlino	non parlino
noi		PRESENT INDICATIVE	
	1st pers. pl.		
		parliamo	non parliamo

80

90

100

110

120

CHAPTER

27

WHAT IS THE SUBJUNCTIVE?

The **SUBJUNCTIVE** is a mood used to express a wish, hope, uncertainty, or other similar attitude toward a fact or an idea. Since it stresses the speaker's feelings about the fact or idea, it expresses a "subjective" point of view.

IN ENGLISH

The subjunctive is only used in very few constructions. Moreover, it is usually difficult to distinguish the forms of the subjunctive from other forms of the verb conjugation.

I *am* in Detroit right now.

present indicative of *to be*

I wish I *were* in Rome right now.

subjunctive same as past tense of *to be*

He *reads* a book each week.

present indicative of *to read*

The professor insists that he *read* a book each week.

subjunctive same as dictionary form of *to read*

The subjunctive occurs most commonly in the subordinate clause (see p. 142) of three kinds of sentences.

- in clauses introduced by *if,* to express conditions contrary-to-fact

| if-condition | result clause |

If I *were* in Europe now, I would buy a villa in Florence.

subjunctive (same as past tense)

- in statements expressing a wish that is not possible

I wish he *were* here with us.

subjunctive (same as past tense)

- following verbs of asking, demanding, and requesting

I asked that Maria *be* present.

subjunctive (same as dictionary form)

IN ITALIAN

The subjunctive, called the **congiuntivo**, is used very frequently. It has four tenses (**presente, passato, imperfetto, trapassato**) whose forms you must learn.

The use of the **congiuntivo** corresponds to the use of the subjunctive in English only in a few cases.

■ in clauses introduced by **se** *if,* to express conditions contrary-to-fact

Se **fossi** ricco, comprerei una villa a Firenze.
*If I **were** rich, I would buy a villa in Florence.*

■ following expressions of wish using **magari** *if only*

Magari **fosse** qui con noi!
*I wish he **were** here with us!*

■ following verbs of command (asking, demanding, etc.)

Esigo che Maria **sia** presente.
*I demand that Maria **be** present.*

As you will see below, when the main clause contains a specific type of verb or expressions, the verb of the subsequent subordinate clause is put in the **congiuntivo**. Note that the English equivalent of the **congiuntivo** is varied and never subjunctive.

■ main clause contains a verb of emotion, wish, command, opinion, doubt → **che** *that* + subjunctive

Temo che Marco non **arrivi** in tempo.
verb of emotion   present subjunctive
present indicative
*I **am afraid that** Marco **will** not **arrive** on time.*
                          future

Teresa **vuole che** il marito **cucini.**
verb of wish   present subjunctive
present indicative
*Teresa **wants** her husband **to cook.***
                    infinitive

Pensiamo che mamma **abbia** ragione.
verb of opinion   present subjunctive
present indicative
*We **think that** Mother **is** right.*
                    present indicative

Dubito che vinciate la partita.
verb of doubt   present subjunctive
present indicative
*I **doubt that** you **will win** the game.*
                    future

■ impersonal verbs or expressions of emotion, wish, command, opinion, doubt → **che** *that* + subjunctive

Sembra che i miei amici **partano** presto per l'Europa.

impersonal verb   present subjunctive
present indicative

*It seems that my friends **are leaving** soon for Europe.*

present progressive indicative

È possibile che papà **compri** una macchina nuova.

impersonal expression   present subjunctive
present indicative

*It is possible that Dad **will buy** a new car.*

future

■ certain conjunctions such as **perchè** *so that*, **a condizione che** *provided that,* etc. → subjunctive

Apriamo la finestra **perchè entri** l'aria fresca.

present   conjunction   present subjunctive
indicative

*We are opening the window **so (that)** fresh air **comes in**.*

present indicative

Ti do il libro **a condizione che** tu me lo **restituisca** presto.

present indicative   conjunction   present subjunctive

*I will give you the book **provided (that)** you **return** it to me soon.*

present indicative

Study your textbook carefully for other uses of the subjunctive and its various tenses.

WHAT IS THE CONDITIONAL?

The CONDITIONAL is not found in English grammar books as a
separate mood, but there is a mood in Italian called **condizionale** (see *What is Meant by Mood?*, p. 47). However, there
are verb forms in English which function in the same way as
the **condizionale**. For practical purposes, we can call these
forms the "present conditional" and the "past conditional."

PRESENT CONDITIONAL
IN ENGLISH

The present conditional is a compound tense. It is formed
with the auxiliary *would* + the dictionary form of the main
verb: *I would like, they would close, we would buy.*

The present conditional is used in the following ways:

- to express polite wishes, requests, and preferences

    I *would like* to eat.
    Would you please lend me your book?
    I *would prefer* not to talk about it.

- in the MAIN CLAUSE of a contrary-to-fact hypothetical
  statement in the present

    I *would buy* a Ferrari, if I were rich,

"I would buy a Ferrari" is a CLAUSE because it is composed
of a group of words containing a subject *(I)* and a verb
(would buy) and is used as part of a sentence. It is the MAIN
CLAUSE because it expresses a complete thought and could
stand by itself. It is also called the RESULT CLAUSE because it
expresses what would happen as the result of being rich.

"If I were rich" is also a clause because it contains a subject *(I)* and a verb *(were)* and is used as part of a sentence.
However, it is a SUBORDINATE CLAUSE, or IF-CLAUSE, because it
does not express a complete thought and cannot stand
alone. It is always found with a main clause.

The entire statement is called CONTRARY-TO-FACT because
it refers to a condition that does not exist, i.e., the person
speaking is not rich, and it is HYPOTHETICAL because the
speaker is speculating, i.e., the person speaking could be
rich one day.

1

10

20

30

■ in an indirect statement to express a FUTURE-IN-THE-PAST

An INDIRECT STATEMENT repeats, or reports, but does not quote, someone's words, as opposed to a DIRECT STATEMENT which is a word-for-word quotation of what someone said. In written form a direct statement is always between quotation marks.

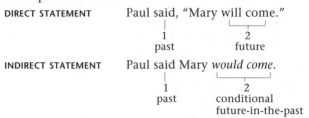

In the indirect statement, action 2 is called a FUTURE-IN-THE-PAST because it takes place after another action in the past, action 1. In the direct statement, action 2 is merely a quotation of what was said.

CAREFUL — The auxiliary *would* does not correspond to the conditional when it stands for *used to*, as in "She *would talk* while he painted." In this sentence, it means *used to talk* and requires the imperfect (see pp. 65-6).

IN ITALIAN

The present conditional, called the **condizionale**, is a simple tense formed with the future stem (see p. 70) + a regular set of endings: (io) parler**ei**, (tu) legger**esti**, (lui) finir**ebbe**, etc. Your textbook will provide all of the forms and irregularities.

As in English, the **condizionale** is used in the following ways:

■ to express polite wishes, requests, and preferences

Vorrei mangiare.
present conditional
I would like to eat.

Mi **presteresti** il tuo libro, per piacere?
present conditional
Would you please lend me your book?

Preferirei non parlarne.
present conditional
I would prefer not to talk about it.

■ in the main clause of a hypothetical statement which is contrary-to-fact at the present time

Se fossi ricco, **comprerei** una Ferrari.
present conditional
*If I were rich, **I would buy** a Ferrari.* 80

Although the statement is contrary-to-fact at the present time, there is the possibility of the condition being fulfilled some time in the future, i.e., if you ever get rich you'll buy a Ferrari.

PAST CONDITIONAL
IN ENGLISH

The past conditional is formed with the auxiliary *would have* + the past participle of the main verb: *I would have liked, they would have closed, we would have bought.* 90

The past conditional is used in the main clause of a hypothetical statement which is contrary-to-fact in the past.

If I had been rich, I *would have bought* a Ferrari.
Contrary-to-fact: I did not buy a Ferrari because I was not rich.

The condition was not fulfilled in the past and the result cannot be changed, i.e, you were not rich and you did not buy a Ferrari.

IN ITALIAN

The past conditional, called the **condizionale passato**, is 100 formed with the auxiliary **avere** *to have* or **essere** *to be* in the present conditional + the past participle of the main verb: **mi sarebbe piaciuto** *I would have liked,* **avrebbero chiuso** *they would have closed,* **avremmo comprato** *we would have bought.*

As in English, the **condizionale passato** is used in the main clause of a contrary-to-fact hypothetical statement in the past.

Se fossi stato ricco, **avrei comprato** una Ferrari.
past conditional 110
*If I had been rich, **I would have bought** a Ferrari.*
past conditional

Unlike English which uses the present conditional to express the future-in-the-past in indirect statements, Italian uses the past conditional.

Paolo ha detto che Maria **sarebbe venuta**.
past conditional
*Paul said that Mary **would come**.*
present conditional 120

SEQUENCE OF TENSES IN HYPOTHETICAL STATEMENTS

Let us study some examples of constructions with conditions and their results so that you learn to recognize them and to use the appropriate tense in Italian.

Hypothetical and contrary-to-fact statements are easy to recognize because they are made up of two clauses:

- the IF-CLAUSE; that is, the subordinate clause introduced by *if* (**se** in Italian)

- the RESULT CLAUSE; that is, the main clause (see p. 81)

If you have difficulty recognizing tenses, just apply these three rules.

1. a hypothetical statement which expresses a possibility

IF-CLAUSE		RESULT CLAUSE	
present tense	+	future tense	ENGLISH
present tense	+	present tense	} ITALIAN
future tense	+	future tense	}

If I have the money, I will come.
    present   future

Se **ho** i soldi, **vengo**.
  present   present

Se **avrò** i soldi, **verrò**.
  future   future

2. a hypothetical statement contrary-to-fact

  a) in the present (fulfillment of the condition is possible)

IF-CLAUSE		RESULT CLAUSE	
simple past	+	present conditional	ENGLISH
imperfect subjunctive	+	present conditional	ITALIAN

If I had the money, I would come.
    past   present conditional

Se **avessi** i soldi, **verrei**.
  imperfect   present conditional
  subjunctive

  b) in the past (fulfillment of the condition was impossible)

IF-CLAUSE		RESULT CLAUSE	
past perfect	+	past conditional	ENGLISH
past perfect subjunctive	+	past conditional	ITALIAN

If I had had the money, I would have come.
  past perfect   past conditional

Se **avessi avuto** i soldi, **sarei venuto**.
  past perfect subjunctive past conditional

SUMMARY

Here is a reference chart of the sequence of tenses (numbers refer to three rules on preceding page).

170

	ENGLISH	ITALIAN
POSSIBLE (1)	**"if" clause** **+ result clause** present + future	**"if" clause** **+ result clause** present + present OR future + future
contrary-to-fact present (2a)	simple past + present conditional	imperfect subjunctive + present conditional
IMPOSSIBLE **contrary-to-fact past (2b)**	past perfect + past conditional	past perfect subjunctive + past conditional

CHAPTER

29

WHAT IS A REFLEXIVE VERB?

A **REFLEXIVE VERB** is a verb conjugated with a special pronoun called a **REFLEXIVE PRONOUN** which serves to "reflect" the action of the verb on the performer or subject.

> *He* sees *himself* in the mirror.
> *We* see *ourselves* in the mirror.

IN ENGLISH

Many verbs can take on a reflexive meaning by adding a reflexive pronoun.

> Paul *cut* the paper.

regular verb

> Paul *cut himself* when he shaved.

verb + reflexive pronoun

Pronouns ending with *-self* or *-selves* are used to make verbs reflexive. Here are the reflexive pronouns.

		SUBJECT PRONOUN	REFLEXIVE PRONOUN
SINGULAR			
1ˢᵗ person		I	myself
2ⁿᵈ person		you	yourself
3ʳᵈ person	he	himself
	she	herself
	it	itself
PLURAL			
1ˢᵗ person		we	ourselves
2ⁿᵈ person		you	yourselves
3ʳᵈ person		they	themselves

In a sentence, the subject and the reflexive pronoun refer to the same person. Notice the word order in English, the subject precedes the verb and the reflexive pronoun follows the verb.

> *I* cut *myself.*

1ˢᵗ person singular

> *The rabbit* tore *itself* free.

3ʳᵈ person singular

Paul and Mary blamed *themselves* for the accident.

3rd person plural

Although the subject pronoun *you* is the same in the singular and plural, the reflexive pronouns are different: *yourself* is used when you are speaking to one person (singular) and *yourselves* is used when you are speaking to more than one (plural).

Paul, did *you* hurt *yourself?*

2nd person singular

Children, did *you* hurt *yourselves?*

2nd person plural

IN ITALIAN

As in English, many regular verbs can be turned into reflexive verbs by adding a reflexive pronoun. Reflexive verbs have an infinitive form which has the reflexive pronoun **si** attached to it: **lavarsi** *to wash oneself.*

Roberto **lava** la macchina.
Robert **washes** *the car.*

Roberto **si lava**.
Robert **washes** *himself.*

The dictionary lists **lavare** as the infinitive of *to wash* and **lavarsi** as the infinitive of *to wash oneself.* You will have to memorize the conjugation of the reflexive verbs with the reflexive pronoun.

Here are the reflexive pronouns in Italian.

mi	*myself*
ti	*yourself* [fam. sing.]
si	*himself, herself, itself, yourself* [form. sing.]
ci	*ourselves*
vi	*yourselves* [fam. pl.]
si	*themselves, yourselves* [form. pl.]

Since the reflexive pronoun reflects the action of the verb back to the performer, the reflexive pronoun will change as the subject of the verb changes. Unlike English, where the reflexive pronoun is placed after the verb, in Italian the reflexive pronoun is usually placed immediately before the verb.

For example, the verb **lavarsi** is conjugated in the present indicative as follows:

SINGULAR	SUBJECT PRONOUN	REFLEXIVE PRONOUN	VERB FORM
1st person	io	mi	lavo
2nd person	tu	ti	lavi
3rd person [form. sing.]	lui / lei / Lei	si	lava
PLURAL			
1st person	noi	ci	laviamo
2nd person	voi	vi	lavate
3rd person [form. pl.]	loro / Loro	si	lavano

Reflexive verbs can be conjugated in all tenses. The subject pronoun and reflexive pronoun remain the same regardless of the verb tense; only the verb form changes: **lui si laverà** *he will wash himself,* **lui si è lavato** *he washed himself.*

The perfect tenses of reflexive verbs are always conjugated with the auxiliary **essere** *to be;* consequently the past participle agrees in gender and number with the subject (see pp. 64-5).

I bambini **si sono lavati.**
*The children **washed (themselves).***
Maria **si è lavata** in fretta.
*Mary **washed (herself)** in a hurry.*

CAREFUL — Reflexive verbs are more common in Italian than in English; that is, there are many English verbs whose Italian equivalent requires a reflexive pronoun. For example, in English when you say "Mary got up," it is understood, but not stated, that she "got *herself* up." In Italian you must express *to get up* with the verb **alzare** *to raise* + the reflexive pronoun **si** *oneself*: **Maria si è alzata.**

In addition, there are many verbal expressions which do not have a reflexive even understood in English, but whose Italian equivalent is a reflexive verb: *to fall in love* **innamorarsi**, *to feel* **sentirsi**, *to notice* **accorgersi**, among others.

WHAT IS MEANT BY ACTIVE AND PASSIVE VOICE?

The **VOICE** of the verb refers to a basic relationship between the verb and its subject. There are two voices: active and passive.

THE ACTIVE VOICE — A sentence is said to be in the active voice when the subject is the performer of the action of the verb. In this instance, the verb is in the **ACTIVE VOICE**.

The teacher *writes* the exam.
subject   verb   direct object

Paul *ate* an apple.
subject verb   direct object

Lightning *has struck* the tree.
subject   verb   direct object

In the above examples, the subject performs the action of the verb and the direct object is the receiver of the action.

THE PASSIVE VOICE — A sentence is said to be in the passive voice when the subject is the receiver of the action. In this instance, the verb is in the **PASSIVE VOICE**.

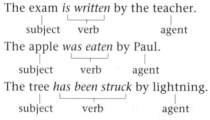

The exam *is written* by the teacher.
subject   verb   agent

The apple *was eaten* by Paul.
subject   verb   agent

The tree *has been struck* by lightning.
subject   verb   agent

In the above examples, the subject is having the action of the verb performed upon it. The performer of the action, if it is mentioned, is introduced by the word *by*. The performer is called the **AGENT**.

IN ENGLISH

The passive voice is expressed by the verb *to be* conjugated in the appropriate tense + the past participle of the main verb (see p. 60). The tense of the passive sentence is indicated by the tense of the verb *to be*.

The exam *is written* by the teacher.

present

The exam *was written* by the teacher.

past

The exam *will be written* by the teacher.

future

IN ITALIAN

As in English, the passive voice can be expressed by the auxiliary verb **essere** *to be* conjugated in the appropriate tense + the past participle of the main verb. The tense of the passive sentence is indicated by the tense of the verb **essere**. The agent is introduced by **da**.

L'esame **è** preparato dal professore.

present
The exam is written by the teacher.

L'esame **è stato** preparato dal professore.

passato prossimo
The exam was written by the teacher.

L'esame **sarà** preparato dal professore.

future
The exam will be written by the teacher.

Because the auxiliary in the passive voice is always **essere**, all past participles in a passive sentence agree in gender and number with the subject (see pp. 64-5).

I **vini** italiani sono **apprezzati** da tutti.

masc. pl.   masc. pl.
Italian wines are appreciated by everyone.

Avoiding the passive voice in Italian

Although the Italian language has a passive voice, it is not used as often as it is in English. Whenever possible, and particularly when the agent does not need to be emphasized, Italian tends to avoid the passive construction by using the active voice, or by using the **si**-construction.

The **si**-construction is composed of the word **si** + the verb in the 3rd person + the subject. The verb will in the 3rd person singular if the subject is singular, and 3rd person plural if the subject is plural.

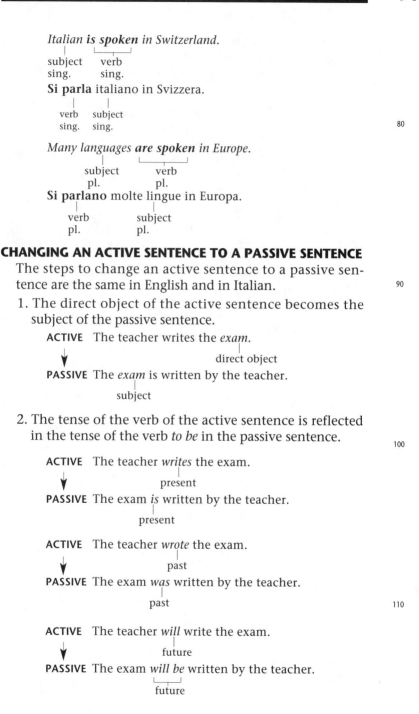

*Italian **is spoken** in Switzerland.*

subject   verb
sing.   sing.

Si parla italiano in Svizzera.

verb   subject
sing.   sing.

*Many languages **are spoken** in Europe.*

subject   verb
pl.   pl.

Si parlano molte lingue in Europa.

verb   subject
pl.   pl.

CHANGING AN ACTIVE SENTENCE TO A PASSIVE SENTENCE

The steps to change an active sentence to a passive sentence are the same in English and in Italian.

1. The direct object of the active sentence becomes the subject of the passive sentence.

    ACTIVE The teacher writes the *exam.*

                              direct object

    PASSIVE The *exam* is written by the teacher.

                subject

2. The tense of the verb of the active sentence is reflected in the tense of the verb *to be* in the passive sentence.

    ACTIVE The teacher *writes* the exam.

                           present

    PASSIVE The exam *is* written by the teacher.

                present

    ACTIVE The teacher *wrote* the exam.

                           past

    PASSIVE The exam *was* written by the teacher.

                past

    ACTIVE The teacher *will* write the exam.

                           future

    PASSIVE The exam *will be* written by the teacher.

                future

3. The subject of the active sentence becomes the agent of the passive sentence introduced with *by*.

ACTIVE   The *teacher* writes the exam.

             subject

PASSIVE The exam is written by the *teacher*.

                            agent

Italian follows the same steps to change a sentence from active voice to passive voice.

ACTIVE   Il professore **prepara** l'esame.

             subject   verb   direct object

             *The **teacher** writes the exam.*

PASSIVE L'esame **è preparato** dal professore.

             subject   verb   agent

             *The exam **is written** by the teacher.*

WHAT IS AN ADJECTIVE?

An ADJECTIVE is a word that describes a noun or a pronoun. The adjective is said to modify the noun or pronoun.

IN ENGLISH

Adjectives are classified according to the way they modify a noun or pronoun.

Descriptive adjective — A descriptive adjective indicates a quality; it describes the characteristics of the noun or pronoun (see p. 94).

> She read an *interesting* book.
> He has *brown* eyes.

Possessive adjective — A possessive adjective indicates ownership of or relationship to a noun (see p. 100).

> *His* book is lost.
> *Our* parents are away.

Interrogative adjective — An interrogative adjective asks a question about someone or something (see p. 105).

> *Which* teachers did you speak to?
> *What* book is lost?

Demonstrative adjective — A demonstrative adjective points out someone or something (see p. 107).

> *This* teacher is excellent.
> We went to Naples *that* summer.

IN ITALIAN

Adjectives are classified in the same way as in English. The principal difference is that in English adjectives generally do not change their form, while Italian adjectives must agree in gender and number with the noun or pronoun they modify.

CHAPTER

32

WHAT IS A DESCRIPTIVE ADJECTIVE?

A **DESCRIPTIVE ADJECTIVE** is a word that indicates a quality of a noun or pronoun. As the name implies, it *describes* the noun or pronoun.

Tina bought a *pretty* dress. It is bright *red*.

adjective
describing
noun *dress*

adjective
describing
pronoun *it*

IN ENGLISH

The descriptive adjective does not change form, regardless of the noun or pronoun it modifies.

Mary bought an *expensive* book.

singular noun described

Mary bought *expensive* books.

plural noun described

In the above examples, the adjective *expensive* has the same form although in one instance it modifies a singular noun and in the other a plural noun.

Descriptive adjectives are divided into two groups depending on how they are connected to the noun they modify.

An **ATTRIBUTIVE ADJECTIVE** is connected directly to its noun and always precedes it.

My family lives in a *white* house.

attributive   noun described
adjective

Good children are praised.

attributive noun described
adjective

A **PREDICATE ADJECTIVE** is connected to the noun, or pronoun, it modifies by a linking verb, usually a form of *to be*. Other common linking verbs are: *to seem, to feel, to smell, to sound, to taste, to become*. The noun or pronoun modified by a predicate adjective is always the subject.

My house is *white*.

noun   predicate adjective
subject
linking verb

They are *good*.

pronoun   predicate adjective
subject

40

IN ITALIAN

Descriptive adjectives are classified in the same way as in English. The important difference is that adjectives, attributive and predicate, agree with the noun or pronoun they modify. Thus, the ending of an adjective changes depending on whether the noun or pronoun is masculine or feminine, singular or plural.

- masculine singular final **-o** → plural final **-i**
- feminine singular final **-a** → plural final **-e**
- masculine and feminine singular final **-e** → plural final **-i**

50

the *red* dress   il vestito **rosso**

masc.   masc.
sing.   sing.

the *red* car   la macchina **rossa**

fem.   fem.
sing.   sing.

the *red* dresses   i vestiti **rossi**

masc. masc.
pl.   pl.

60

the *red* cars   le macchine **rosse**

fem.   fem.
pl.   pl.

As you can see in the English examples above, the attributive adjective *red* precedes the noun it modifies; whereas, in Italian, **rosso** follows the noun. Some Italian attributive adjectives precede the noun they modify, such as the commonly used attributive adjective **buono** *good*.

I **buoni** bambini sono lodati.

adjective   noun

70

Good children are praised.

Your textbook will indicate which Italian attributive adjectives follow the noun they modify and which precede it.

Predicate adjectives always follow the linking verb and agree with the subject.

I bambini sono **buoni**.

subject   linking adjective
          verb
          └─ masc. pl. ─┘

80

The children are *good*.

Lei è **ricca**; lui è **povero**.

pronoun adj. pronoun adj.
subject   subject

⌊ fem. sing. ⌋ ⌊ masc. sing. ⌋

*She is **rich**; he is **poor**.*

NOUNS USED AS ADJECTIVES

IN ENGLISH

You should be able to recognize nouns used as adjectives; that is, a noun used to modify another noun. When a noun is used to describe another noun, the structure is as follows: the describing noun (i.e., the noun used as an adjective) + the noun described.

Leather is expensive.   *Leather* goods are expensive.

noun   noun   noun described
                              used as adjective

The desk is black.   The *desk* lamp is black.

noun   noun   noun described
                              used as adjective

IN ITALIAN

When a noun is used as an adjective, that is, to describe another noun, it remains a noun with its own gender and number; it does not agree with the noun described. The structure is as follows: the noun described + a preposition (normally **in, da**, or **di**) + the describing noun.

leather goods   prodotti **in pelle**

noun   noun
masc. pl.   fem. sing.

desk lamp   lampada **da tavolo**

noun   noun
fem. sing.   masc. sing.

WHAT IS MEANT BY COMPARISON OF ADJECTIVES?

We compare adjectives when two or more nouns have the   1
same quality (height, size, color, or any other characteristic)
and we want to indicate that one of these nouns has a
greater, lesser, or equal degree of this quality.[1]

comparison of adjectives
Paul is *tall* but Mary is *taller*.

adjective   adjective
modifies *Paul*   modifies *Mary*

In both English and Italian there are two types of comparison: the comparative and the superlative.   10

COMPARATIVE
The comparative is used to compare the quality of one noun
to the quality of another noun. There are three degrees of
comparison.

IN ENGLISH
Greater degree — The comparison of greater degree
(more) is formed differently depending on the length of
the adjective being compared.

- short adjective + *-er* + *than*   20
  Paul is *taller than* Mary.
  Susan is *older than* her sister.

- *more* + longer adjective + *than*
  Mary is *more intelligent than* John.
  My car is *more expensive than* your car.

Lesser degree — The comparison of lesser degree (less) is
formed as follows: *less* + adjective + *than.*
  John is *less intelligent than* Mary.
  Your car is *less old than* my car.

Equal degree — The comparison of equal degree (same) is   30
formed as follows: *as* + adjective + *as.*
  Paul is *as tall as* John.
  My car is *as expensive as* his car.

---

[1]In English and in Italian the structure for comparing adverbs (see *What is
an Adverb?*, p. 109) is the same as the structure for comparing adjectives.

IN ITALIAN

Greater degree — The comparison of greater degree is formed as follows: **più** + adjective + **di**.

Giovanni è **più alto di** Roberto.
*John is **taller than** Robert.*

La mia macchina è **più cara della** tua macchina.
*My car is **more expensive than** your car.*

Lesser degree — The comparison of lesser degree is formed as follows: **meno** + adjective + **di**.

Roberto è **meno alto di** Giovanni.
*Robert is **less tall than** John.*

La tua macchina è **meno cara della** mia macchina.
*Your car is **less expensive than** my car.*

Equal degree — The comparison of equal degree is formed as follows: **(tanto)** + adjective + **quanto** or **(così)** + adjective + **come**.

Giovanni è **(tanto) alto quanto** Roberto.
Giovanni è **(così) alto come** Roberto.
*John is **as tall as** Robert.*

La mia macchina è **(tanto) cara quanto** la tua macchina.
La mia macchina è **(così) cara come** la tua macchina.
*My car is **as expensive as** your car.*

SUPERLATIVE: RELATIVE AND ABSOLUTE SUPERLATIVE

The RELATIVE SUPERLATIVE is the highest or lowest degree of a quality as compared to more than one person or thing.

IN ENGLISH

Highest degree — The relative superlative of highest degree is formed differently depending on the length of the adjectives:

- *the* + short adjective + *-est*

    John is *the tallest* of three brothers.
    My car is *the cheapest* on the market.

- *the most* + long adjective

    Mary is *the most intelligent* in the class.
    My car is *the most expensive* in the race.

Lowest degree — The relative superlative of lowest degree is formed as follows: *the least* + adjective.

Robert is *the least tall* of his three brothers.
My car is *the least expensive* in the race.

IN ITALIAN

Highest degree — The relative superlative of highest degree is formed as follows: the definite article + **più** + adjective + **di.**   80

Giovanni è **il più alto dei** tre fratelli.
John is the tallest of the three brothers.

Questo bambino è **il più intelligente della** classe.
This child is the most intelligent in the class.

Lowest degree — The relative superlative of lowest degree is formed as follows: the definite article + **meno** + adjective + **di.**

Roberto è **il meno alto dei** tre fratelli.
Robert is the least tall of the three brothers.   90

La mia macchina è **la meno cara della** corsa.
My car is the least expensive in the race.

The **ABSOLUTE SUPERLATIVE** is the highest degree of a quality without comparison to any other person or thing.

IN ENGLISH

The absolute superlative is formed by placing an intensifying adverb such as *very, extremely* + adjective.

Dennis is *very tall.*
My car is *extremely expensive.*   100

IN ITALIAN

The absolute superlative is usually formed as follows: adjective + **-issimo** or with **molto** *very,* **estremamente** *extremely,* **assolutamente** *absolutely* + adjective.

Dennis è **altissimo.**
*Dennis is **very tall.***

La mia macchina è **estremamente cara.**
*My car is **extremely expensive.***

CAREFUL — In English and in Italian a few adjectives have irregular forms of comparison which you will have to memorize individually.   110

ADJECTIVE	*This apple is **bad**.*
	Questa mela è **cattiva.**
COMPARATIVE	*This apple is **worse*** [not *badder*].
	Questa mela è **più cattiva.**
	Questa mela è **peggiore.**
SUPERLATIVE	*This apple is **the worst*** [not *the baddest*].
	Questa mela è **la più cattiva.**
	Questa mela è **la peggiore.**

WHAT IS A POSSESSIVE ADJECTIVE?

A **POSSESSIVE ADJECTIVE** is a word that indicates ownership of, or relationship to, the noun it modifies. The owner is called the *possessor* and the noun modified is called the person or thing *possessed*.

Whose house is that? It's *my* house.

possessor   noun
possessed

My uncle is a lawyer.

IN ENGLISH

Here are the forms of the possessive adjectives:

SINGULAR

1ˢᵗ person		my
2ⁿᵈ person		your
3ʳᵈ person	masc.	his
	fem.	her
	neuter	its

PLURAL

1ˢᵗ person	our
2ⁿᵈ person	your
3ʳᵈ person	their

Possessive adjectives refer to the possessor.

What color is John's car? *His* car is white.

possessor singular

What color is the Smiths' car? *Their* car is white.

possessor plural

Although the object possessed is the same, *car,*
the possessive adjective varies to agree with the possessor:
John → singular *(his)*, *the Smiths* → plural *(their).*

Possessive adjectives never change their form, regardless of the thing possessed.

Mary is reading *my* magazine.

object possessed singular

Mary is reading *my* magazines.

object possessed plural

Although the objects possessed are different in number (magazine → singular; magazines → plural), the possessive adjective is the same, *my.*

IN ITALIAN

As in English, an Italian possessive adjective refers to the possessor, but unlike English, it must agree, like all Italian adjectives, in gender and number with the noun it modifies, that is, the person or object possessed. Also, Italian normally uses the definite article before the possessive adjective. Therefore, the gender and number of the person or object possessed is reflected in both the definite article and the possessive adjective.

> *Maria is reading **my** magazine.*
> Maria sta leggendo **la** mia rivista.

object possessed
fem. sing.

definite possessive
article adjective

└ fem. sing. ┘

The possessive adjective **mia** is feminine singular to agree with the feminine singular noun **rivista**.

> *Maria is reading **my** magazines.*
> Maria sta leggendo **le** mie riviste.

object possessed
fem. pl.

definite possessive
article adjective

└ fem. pl. ┘

The possessive adjective **mie** is feminine plural to agree with the feminine plural noun **riviste**.

These are the steps you should follow in order to choose the correct possessive adjective and its proper form:

1. GENDER & NUMBER OF NOUN POSSESSED — Identify the gender and number of the person(s) or item(s) possessed.

2. POSSESSOR — Identify the possessor. Except for **loro** and **Loro** the possessor is shown by the first few letters of the possessive adjective.

my	**mi-**
your [fam. sing.]	**tu-**
his, her, its	**su-**
your [formal sing.]	**Su-**
our	**nostr-**
your [fam. pl.]	**vostr-**
their	**loro**
your [formal pl.]	**Loro**

3. DEFINITE ARTICLE — Depending on the gender and number of the noun possessed, place the appropriate definite article before the possessive adjective (see pp. 16-7 in *What is an Article?*).

4. ENDING — Depending on the gender and number of the noun possessed, add the appropriate ending to the possessive adjective (except for **loro** and **Loro** which are invariable).

SINGULAR
masculine $\rightarrow$ -o
feminine $\rightarrow$ -a

PLURAL
masculine $\rightarrow$ -i (except for **mi-** which adds -ei, and
                              tu-, **su-**, and **Su-** which add -oi)
feminine $\rightarrow$ -e

5. SELECTION — The definite article + the possessive adjective + the noun possessed should agree in gender and number.

Below are examples of how these steps are applied to sentences with each possible possessor.

"My"

*I have **my** books.*
1. GENDER AND NUMBER OF NOUN POSSESSED:
   Libri *books* is masculine plural.
2. POSSESSOR: my   **mi-**
3. & 4. DEFINITE ARTICLE & ENDING: **i + -ei**
5. SELECTION: **i miei libri**

Ho **i miei** libri.

"Your" — In the case of the possessive adjective *your*, you will have to consider additional factors:

a. FAMILIAR OR FORMAL — Is the familiar or formal form of address appropriate (see pp. 32-4)?

b. NUMBER — Does *your* address one person (singular) or more than one person (plural)?

*Is this **your** house?* [addressing a child]
1. GENDER AND NUMBER OF NOUN POSSESSED:
   Casa *house* is feminine singular.
2. POSSESSOR: your
   a. FORMAL OR FAMILIAR: familiar
   b. SINGULAR OR PLURAL: singular   **tu-**
3. & 4. DEFINITE ARTICLE & ENDING: **la + -a**
5. SELECTION: **la tua casa**

È questa **la tua** casa?

*Is this **your** house?* [addressing more than one child]
   1. GENDER AND NUMBER OF NOUN POSSESSED:
   Casa *house* is feminine singular.
   2. POSSESSOR: your
      a. FORMAL OR FAMILIAR: familiar
      b. SINGULAR OR PLURAL: plural   **vostr-**
   3. & 4. DEFINITE ARTICLE & ENDING: **la + -a**
   5. SELECTION: **la vostra casa**
È questa **la vostra** casa?

*Is this **your** house?* [addressing an unfamiliar adult]
   1. GENDER AND NUMBER OF NOUN POSSESSED:
   Casa *house* is feminine singular.
   2. POSSESSOR: your
      a. FORMAL OR FAMILIAR: formal
      b. SINGULAR OR PLURAL: singular   **Su-**
   3. & 4. DEFINITE ARTICLE & ENDING: **la + -a**
   5. SELECTION: **la Sua casa**
È questa **la Sua** casa?

*Is this **your** house?* [addressing more than one unfamiliar adult]
   1. GENDER AND NUMBER OF NOUN POSSESSED:
   Casa *house* is feminine singular.
   2. POSSESSOR: your
      a. FORMAL OR FAMILIAR: formal
      b. SINGULAR OR PLURAL: plural   **Loro**
   3. DEFINITE ARTICLE: **la**
   4. SELECTION: **la Loro casa**
È questa **la Loro** casa?

Since **Loro** is invariable, the gender and number of the possessive adjective are only indicated by the definite article.

"His, her, its" — Since Italian possessive adjectives only agree with the noun possessed and do not identify the gender of the possessor, when translating into English you will have to rely on context to determine whether *his, her* or *its* is the appropriate possessive adjective.

*Mary reads **her** books.*
   1. GENDER AND NUMBER OF NOUN POSSESSED:
   Libri *books* is masculine plural.
   2. POSSESSOR: her   **su-**
   3. & 4. DEFINITE ARTICLE & ENDING: **i + -oi**
   5. SELECTION: **i suoi libri**
Maria legge **i suoi** libri.

*Mario reads **his** books.*
   1. GENDER AND NUMBER OF POSSESSED:
   Libri *books* is masculine plural.
   2. POSSESSOR: his   **su-**
   3. & 4. DEFINITE ARTICLE & ENDING: **i + -oi**
   5. SELECTION: **i suoi libri**
Mario legge **i suoi** libri.

120

130

140

150

160

"Our"

Our house is downtown.
1. GENDER AND NUMBER OF NOUN POSSESSED:
   Casa *house* is feminine singular.
2. POSSESSOR: our   nostr-
3. & 4. DEFINITE ARTICLE & ENDING: la + -a
5. SELECTION: **la nostra casa**

La nostra casa è in centro.

"Their" — Since **loro** is invariable, the gender and number of the possessive adjective are indicated only by the definite article.

*This is **their** house.*
1. GENDER AND NUMBER OF NOUN POSSESSED:
   Casa *house* is feminine singular.
2. POSSESSOR: their   loro
3. DEFINITE ARTICLE: la
4. SELECTION: **la loro casa**

Questa è **la loro** casa.

*These are **their** houses.*
1. GENDER AND NUMBER OF NOUN POSSESSED:
   Case *houses* is feminine plural.
2. POSSESSOR: their   loro
3. DEFINITE ARTICLE: le
4. SELECTION: **le loro case**

Queste sono **le loro** case.

SUMMARY

Here is a chart of the possessive adjectives you can use as reference.

	SINGULAR		PLURAL	
POSSESSOR	MASC.	FEM.	MASC.	FEM.
my	il mio	la mia	i miei	le mie
your [fam. sing.]	il tuo	la tua	i tuoi	le tue
his, her, its	il suo	la sua	i suoi	le sue
your [form. sing.]	il Suo	la Sua	i Suoi	le Sue
our	il nostro	la nostra	i nostri	le nostre
your [fam. pl.]	il vostro	la vostra	i vostri	le vostre
their	il loro	la loro	i loro	le loro
your [form. pl.]	il Loro	la Loro	i Loro	le Loro

WHAT IS AN INTERROGATIVE ADJECTIVE?

An **INTERROGATIVE ADJECTIVE** is a word that asks a question about a noun.

Which teacher do you have?

interrogative   noun
adjective

IN ENGLISH

The words *which, what* and *how much, how many* are interrogative adjectives when they precede a noun and are used to ask a question about that noun. (When they are not followed by a noun they are interrogative pronouns, see p. 132.)

What courses are you taking?
Which newspaper do you prefer to read?
How much coffee do you drink?
How many children were there?

IN ITALIAN

There are three interrogative adjectives:

1. to ask a general question: *what* or *which* + noun → **che** + noun

   Che is invariable; it does not agree in gender and number with the noun it modifies.

   Che giornale leggi?
   ***What** newspaper do you read?*

   Che corsi frequenti?
   ***What** courses are you taking?*

2. to ask a question implying a choice between two or more alternatives: *which* or *what* + noun → a form of **quale** + noun

   Quale agrees only in number with the noun it modifies; it does not agree in gender.

   Quale giornale preferisci leggere?

   singular
   ***Which** newspaper do you prefer to read?* [among these three]

   Quali dischi porti?

   plural
   ***Which** records are you bringing?* [among this pile]

3. to ask *how much* or *how many* + noun → a form of **quanto** + noun

40 **Quanto (-a, -i, -e)** has four forms to agree in gender and number with the noun it modifies.

> **Quanto** caffè bevi?
>
> masculine singular
> *How much coffee do you drink?*

> **Quante** valigie porti?
>
> feminine plural
> *How many suitcases are you taking?*

WHAT IS A DEMONSTRATIVE ADJECTIVE?

A DEMONSTRATIVE ADJECTIVE is a word used to indicate whether [1]
a noun is close or distant in space or time.

> *This* book is more interesting than *that* book.
> | | | |
> dem. noun   dem. noun
> adj.   adj.
>
> *This* year the wine is good; *that* year it was terrible.

IN ENGLISH

The demonstrative adjective *this* points out a person or an
object near the speaker and *that* points out a person or an
object away from the speaker. They are a rare example of [10]
adjectives agreeing in number with the noun they modify:
this is used before a singular noun but changes to *these*
before a plural noun and *that* changes to *those*.

> *this* dish   →   *these* dishes
> *that* day   →   *those* days

IN ITALIAN

As in English, there are two sets of demonstrative adjectives: one set for persons or objects close to the speaker,
and one for those far from the speaker. In addition, each
set has four forms which agree in gender and number [20]
with the nouns they modify.

- noun near the speaker: *this, these* → a form of **questo**

> *Do you see **this** boy?*
> > 1. GENDER & NUMBER OF NOUN MODIFIED:
> > **Ragazzo** *boy* is masculine singular.
> > 2. DEMONSTRATIVE ADJECTIVE: masculine singular→ **questo**
>
> Vedi **questo** ragazzo?
>   masc.
>   sing.

> *Do you see **these** houses?* [30]
> > 1. GENDER & NUMBER OF NOUN MODIFIED:
> > **Case** *house* is feminine plural.
> > 2. DEMONSTRATIVE ADJECTIVE: feminine plural → **queste**
>
> Vedi **queste** case?
>   fem.
>   pl.

Here is a chart of the four basic forms of **questo** you can use as a reference.

SINGULAR		
masculine	questo	*this*
feminine	questa	
PLURAL		
masculine	questi	*these*
feminine	queste	

■ noun away from the speaker → a form of **quello**

In addition to the four basic forms depending on the gender and number of the noun modified, a different demonstrative adjective is used depending on the letter, or letters, with which the modified noun begins. (They follow the same pattern as the definite article, pp. 16-7.)

To choose the correct demonstrative adjective establish the following.

1. Gender and number of the noun modified.
2. Beginning letter or letters of the noun modified. There are three possibilities:
   ■ z- or s- + consonant
   ■ any other consonant
   ■ a vowel

Here are some examples:

*Do you see **that** student?*
GENDER & NUMBER & BEGINNING LETTER OF NOUN MODIFIED:
student → **studente** masculine singular, s- + consonant.
Vedi **quello** studente?

*Do you see **those** trees?*
GENDER & NUMBER & BEGINNING LETTER OF NOUN MODIFIED:
trees → **alberi** masculine plural, vowel.
Vedi **quegli** alberi?

Here is a chart of beginning letters of modified nouns and the corresponding form of **quello** you can use as reference.

	Before z- or s- + consonant	Before another consonant	Before a vowel	
SINGULAR				
masculine	quello	quel	quell'	*that*
feminine	quella	quella	quell'	
PLURAL				
masculine	quegli	quei	quegli	*those*
feminine	quelle	quelle	quelle	

WHAT IS AN ADVERB?

An **ADVERB** is a word that describes a verb, an adjective, or
another adverb.[1]

> Mary drives *well*.
>   verb   adverb
>
> The house is *very* big.
>   adverb adjective
>
> The girl ran *too quickly*.
>   adverb adverb

IN ENGLISH

There are different types of adverbs:

- adverbs of manner answer the question *how?* They are
  the most common adverbs and can usually be recognized by their *-ly* ending.

  > Mary sings *beautifully*.
  >   *Beautifully* describes the verb *sings*, how Mary sings.
  >
  > They parked the car *carefully*.
  >   *Carefully* describes the verb *parked*, how the car was parked.

- adverbs of quantity or degree answer the question *how
  much?*

  > Paul is *quite* studious.

- adverbs of time answer the question *when?*

  > He will be home *soon*.

- adverbs of place answer the question *where?*

  > I left my books *there*.

IN ITALIAN

Adverbs must be memorized as vocabulary. The adverbs of
manner can be recognized by their ending **-mente** which
corresponds to the English ending *-ly*.

> natural**mente**   *naturally*
> general**mente**   *generally*
> rapida**mente**   *rapidly*

---

[1]In English and in Italian the structure for comparing adverbs is the same as
the structure for comparing adjectives (see *What is Meant by Comparison of
Adjectives?*, p. 97).

The most important fact for you to remember is that adverbs are invariable; this means that they never become plural, nor do they have gender.

ADVERB OR ADJECTIVE?
IN ENGLISH

You can identify a word as an adverb or adjective by looking at the word modified:
- if it modifies a verb, an adjective, or an adverb → adverb
- if it modifies a noun or a pronoun → adjective

> *The **beautiful** diva sang **beautifully**.*
> Beautiful modifies the noun *diva*; it is an adjective. *Beautifully* modifies the verb *sang*; it describes how she sang; it is an adverb.

IN ITALIAN

It is particularly important to distinguish adverbs from adjectives in Italian since adverbs are invariable, but adjectives must agree with the noun they modify. For example, the word **molto** can be used as an adverb or an adjective.

> *Maria speaks **a lot**.*
> modifies *speak*, a verb → adverb
> Maria parla **molto**.
> adverb (invariable)

> *Maria speaks **very** well.*
> modifies *well*, an adverb → adverb
> Maria parla **molto** bene.
> adverb (invariable)

> *Maria is **very** conscientious.*
> modifies *conscientious*, an adjective → adverb
> Maria è **molto** diligente.
> adverb (invariable)

But:

> *Maria speaks **many** languages.*
> modifies *languages*, a noun → adjective
> Maria parla **molte** lingue.
> adjective   noun
> fem. pl.   fem. pl.

CAREFUL — In colloquial English adjectives are often used instead of adverbs. For instance, we hear "they spoke *loud*" instead of *loudly;* "he drove *slow*" instead of *slowly.* In Italian you don't have a choice, you must use the adverb in these cases.

Remember that in English *good* is an adjective; *well* is an adverb.

> The boy writes *good* English.
> > *Good* modifies the noun *English* → adjective
>
> The student writes *well.*
> > *Well* modifies the verb *writes* → adverb

Likewise, in Italian **buono** is an adjective meaning *good;* **bene** is the adverb meaning *well.*

> *It's a **good** car and it runs **well**.*
> adjective   adverb
> È una **buona** macchina e va **bene.**
> adjective   adverb
> fem. sing.

CHAPTER

38

WHAT IS A PREPOSITION?

A **PREPOSITION** is a word that shows the relationship of one word (usually a verb, a noun or pronoun) to another word in the sentence. The noun or pronoun following the preposition is called the **OBJECT OF THE PREPOSITION**. The preposition plus its object is called a **PREPOSITIONAL PHRASE**.

prepositional phrase

The teacher was *in* the classroom.

object of the preposition

IN ENGLISH

Prepositions normally indicate position, direction, or time.

- prepositions showing position

  Paul was *in* the car.
  Mary put the books *on* the table.

- prepositions showing direction

  Mary went *to* school.
  The students came directly *from* class.

- prepositions showing time

  Italian people go on vacation *in* August.
  Before class, they went to eat.

Not all prepositions are single words:

because of	in front of	instead of
due to	in spite of	on account of

The meaning of a preposition is often determined by its context. Notice the different meanings of the preposition "on" in the following sentences: she lives *on* the floor above, John was *on* time, he spoke *on* writing.

In all the sentences above, the preposition comes before its object. However, the position of a preposition in an English sentence may vary and the preposition may be placed after its object. Spoken English often places a preposition at the end of the sentence; in this position it is called a **DANGLING PREPOSITION**. In formal English we usually try to avoid a dangling preposition by placing it within the sentence before its object or at the beginning of a question (see also pp. 132-3).

SPOKEN ENGLISH → FORMAL ENGLISH
The man I spoke *to* is Italian. The man *to whom* I spoke is
Italian.
Who are you going *with?* *With whom* are you going? 40
Here is the book you asked *about.* Here is the book *about which*
you asked.

IN ITALIAN

You will have to memorize prepositions as vocabulary. As in English, prepositions have a different meaning depending on their context.

There are three important things to remember:

1. Prepositions are invariable. They never become plural, nor do they have a gender. 50
2. Prepositions are tricky. Every language uses prepositions differently. Do not assume that the same preposition is used in Italian as in English, or even that a preposition is used in Italian when one is used in English, and vice versa.

ENGLISH	→	ITALIAN
change of prepositions		
to laugh *at*		ridersi **di** *of*
to be married *to*		essere sposato **con** *with*
same		**different**
preposition		**prepositions**
to go *to* Florence		andare **a** Firenze
to go *to* Italy		andare **in** Italia
to go *to* Luciano's		andare **da** Luciano
preposition		**no preposition**
to look *for*		cercare
to look *at*		guardare
to pay *for*		pagare
no preposition		**preposition**
to approach		avvicinarsi **a**
to enter		entrare **in**

An Italian dictionary will give you the verb plus the preposition when one is required. In the case of an English verb followed by a preposition, be careful not to translate it into Italian word-for-word. For example, to find the word for *to look for*, do not stop at the first dictionary entry for *look* which is **guardare** and then add the preposition *per* corresponding to *for*. Continue searching for the specific expression *look for* which corresponds to the verb **cercare**, used without a preposition (see also p. 25).

80
I am looking for Tina.
Cerco Tina.

On the other hand, when looking up verbs such as *enter, telephone, trust,* be sure to include the Italian preposition which you will you find listed in the dictionary entry.

Mary is entering the classroom.
Maria entra **in** classe.

3. Although in an English sentence the position of a preposition may vary, in Italian the position of a preposition is set: a preposition is always placed within a sentence before its object. There are no dangling prepositions. With regard to the position of prepositions, Italian has the same structure as formal English.

90

*The man I speak **to** is my uncle.* →
*To man **to** whom I speak is my uncle.*
L'uomo **a** cui parlo è mio zio.

*Who are you playing **with**?* →
***With** whom are you playing?*
Con chi giochi?

WHAT IS A CONJUNCTION?

A CONJUNCTION is a word that links words or groups of words.   1

>day *or* night
>He went to sleep *because* he was tired.

IN ENGLISH

There are two kinds of conjunctions: coordinating and subordinating.

COORDINATING CONJUNCTIONS — A coordinating conjunction joins words, phrases, and clauses that are equal; it coordinates elements of equal rank. The major coordinating conjunctions are *and, but, or, neither...nor, for,* and *yet.*   10

>*neither* here *nor* there
>over the river *and* through the woods
>They invited us, *but* we couldn't go.

SUBORDINATING CONJUNCTIONS — A subordinating conjunction joins a dependent clause to a main clause; it subordinates one clause to another (see p. 142). The clause introduced by a subordinating conjunction is called a SUBORDINATE CLAUSE. Typical subordinating conjunctions are *before, after, since, although, because, if, unless, so that, while, that,* and *when.*   20

>*Although* we were invited, we didn't go.
> |
>subordinating   main
>conjunction   clause

>They left *after* the concert ended.
>main   subordinating
>clause   conjunction

>He said *that* he was tired.
>main   subordinating
>clause   conjunction

Notice that the subordinate clause may come before or after the main clause.   30

IN ITALIAN

Conjunctions must be memorized as vocabulary items. Like adverbs and prepositions, conjunctions are invariable; that is, they never change their form.

CAREFUL — In English, the same word may sometimes function as either a subordinating conjunction or a preposition; in Italian, however, a different word would normally be required for each function.

We can distinguish between a subordinating conjunction and a prepostion simply by determining if the word introduces a prepositional phrase (see p. 112) or a subordinate clause.

For instance, *before* can be used as a subordinating conjunction and as a preposition in English. In Italian, however, as a subordinating conjunction *before* is **prima che**, but **prima** as a preposition.

subordinate clause

*We left **before** the intermission began.*

subordinating   subject + verb
conjunction

subordinate clause

Ce ne siamo andati **prima che** cominciasse l'intervallo.

subordinating   verb + subject
conjunction

prepositional phrase

*We left **before** the intermission.*

preposition   object of preposition

prepositional phrase

Ce ne siamo andati **prima** dell'intervallo.

preposition   object of preposition

WHAT IS AN OBJECT?

Every sentence consists, at the very least, of a subject and a verb. This is called the SENTENCE BASE.

1

> John writes.
> She spoke.

The subject of the sentence is usually a noun or pronoun. Many sentences contain other nouns or pronouns that are related to the action of the verb or to a preposition. These nouns or pronouns are called OBJECTS. They indicate the person or persons, or thing or things that receive the action of the verb.

> Paul writes a *letter*.
> subject | object
>   verb

10

> Paul writes *Mary* often.
> subject | object
>   verb

> Paul goes out with her *sister*.
> subject   verb   object

There are three types of objects: direct object, indirect object, and object of a preposition.

20

DIRECT OBJECT
IN ENGLISH

A **DIRECT OBJECT** is a noun or pronoun that receives the action of the verb directly, without a preposition between the verb and the following noun or pronoun. It answers the question *what?* or *whom?* asked after the verb.[1]

> Paul writes *a letter*.
> > QUESTION: Paul writes what? ANSWER: A letter.
> > *A letter* is the direct object.

30

> They see *Paul and Mary*.
> > QUESTION: They see whom? ANSWER: Paul and Mary.
> > *Paul and Mary* are the two direct objects.

Do not assume that any word that comes right after a verb is the direct object. For it to be the direct object it must answer the question *what?* or *whom?*

---

[1]In this section, we will consider active sentences only. (See *What is Meant by Active and Passive Voice?*, p. 89.)

John writes well.

QUESTION: John writes what? ANSWER: No answer.
QUESTION: John writes whom? ANSWER: No answer.
There is no direct object in the sentence.
Well is an adverb; it answers the question: John writes *how*?

Verbs can be classified as to whether or not they take a direct object.

- a **TRANSITIVE VERB** is a verb that takes a direct object

  The boy *threw* the ball.

         transitive verb direct object

- an **INTRANSITIVE VERB** is a verb that does not take a direct object

  Paul *is sleeping*.

      intransitive verb

IN ITALIAN

As in English, a direct object is a noun or pronoun that receives the action of the verb directly, without a preposition.

Giovanni scrive **una lettera**.
*John writes **a letter**.*

Vedono **Paolo e Maria**.
*They see **Paul and Mary**.*

INDIRECT OBJECT
IN ENGLISH

An **INDIRECT OBJECT** is a noun or pronoun that receives the action of the verb indirectly, through the preposition *to* or *for*. It answers the two-word question *to* or *for whom?* or *to* or *for what?* asked after the verb.

John writes *to his brother*.

QUESTION: John writes to whom? ANSWER: To his brother.
His brother is the indirect object.

Sometimes the word *to* is not included in the English sentence.

John writes *his brother*.

IN ITALIAN

As in English, an indirect object is a noun or pronoun that receives the action of the verb indirectly. Nouns that are indirect objects are easy to identify in Italian because they are always preceded by the preposition **a**.

Giovanni scrive **a suo fratello**.
*John writes **his brother**.*

SENTENCES WITH A DIRECT AND INDIRECT OBJECT

A sentence may contain both a direct object and an indirect object.

IN ENGLISH

When a sentence has both a direct and indirect object, the following two word orders are possible:

1. subject (S) + verb (V) + indirect object (IO) + direct object (DO)

Paul gave his sister a gift.
| | | |
S   V   IO   DO

> QUESTION: Who gave a gift? ANSWER: Paul.
> *Paul* is the subject.
> QUESTION: Paul gave what? ANSWER: A gift.
> *A gift* is the direct object.
> QUESTION: Paul gave a gift to whom? ANSWER: His sister.
> *His sister* is the indirect object.

2. subject + verb + direct object + *to* + indirect object

Paul gave a gift to his sister.
| | | | |
S   V   DO *to*   IO

The first structure is the most common. However, because there is no *to* preceding the indirect object, it is more diffi- cult to identify its function than in the second structure. Be sure to ask the questions to establish the function of objects in a sentence.

IN ITALIAN

When a sentence contains both a direct and an indirect object noun, the word order is usually subject + verb + direct object + **a** + indirect object.

Giovanni scrive **una lettera a suo fratello**.
| | | | |
S   V   DO   **a**   IO
John writes a letter to his brother.
John writes his brother a letter.

Notice that in Italian the direct object noun precedes the indirect object noun.

OBJECT OF A PREPOSITION
IN ENGLISH

An OBJECT OF A PREPOSITION is a noun or pronoun that follows a preposition. It answers the question *what?* or *whom?* asked after the preposition. Remember that a personal noun or pronoun following the preposition *to*, how- ever, is usually an indirect object (see p.118).

John went *with Mary*.
> QUESTION: John went with whom? ANSWER: With Mary.
> *Mary* is the object of the preposition *with*.

They entered the house through *the window*.
> QUESTION: They entered through what?
> ANSWER: Through the window.
> *The window* is the object of the preposition *through*.

IN ITALIAN

As in English, an object of a preposition is a noun or pronoun that receives the action of the verb through a preposition other than **a** *to*, which usually precedes an indirect object.

> Giovanni è andato **con Maria**.
> *John went **with Mary**.*

> Sono entrati in casa **dalla finestra**.
> *They entered the house **through the window**.*

CAREFUL — The relationship between verb and object is often different in English and Italian. For example, a verb may take an object of a preposition in English, but a direct object in Italian. It is important that you pay close attention to such differences when you learn Italian verbs. Your textbook, as well as dictionaries, will indicate when an Italian verb is followed by a preposition.

Here are some examples.

- **Object of a preposition in English** → **Direct object in Italian**

  I am looking for the book.
  > FUNCTION IN ENGLISH: object of a preposition
  > QUESTION: I am looking for what? ANSWER: The book.
  > *The book* is the object of the preposition *for*.

  Cerco **il libro**.
  > FUNCTION IN ITALIAN: direct object
  > QUESTION: Che cerco? ANSWER: Il libro.
  > **Il libro** *the book* is a direct object.

  Many common verbs require an object of a preposition in English but a direct object in Italian.

*to look **at***	guardare
*to wait **for***	aspettare
*to pay **for***	pagare

- **Direct object in English** → **Indirect object in Italian**

  *She calls **her friends** every day*.
  > FUNCTION IN ENGLISH: direct object
  > QUESTION: She calls whom? ANSWER: Her friends.
  > *Her friends* is the direct object of *calls*.

Telefona **ai suoi amici** ogni giorno.

Function in Italian: indirect object

Question: A chi telefona ogni giorno? Answer: Ai suoi amici.

Suoi amici *her friends* is an indirect object.

A few common verbs require a direct object in English but an indirect object in Italian.

to obey	obbedire
to resemble	somigliare
to believe	credere

- **Direct object in English → Object of a preposition in Italian**

*Mary's parents remember **the war**.*

Function in English: direct object

Question: Mary's parents remember what? Answer: The war.

The war is the direct object.

I genitori di Maria si ricordano **della guerra**.
di + la

Function in Italian: object of preposition

Question: Di che si ricordano i genitori di Maria?

Answer: Della guerra.

La guerra *the war* is the object of the preposition **di**.

A few common verbs require a direct object in English but an object of a preposition in Italian.

to enter	entrare **in**
to trust	fidarsi **di**
to doubt	dubitare **di**

- **Subject in English → Indirect object in Italian**

With some Italian verbs (v), the equivalent of a subject (s) in English is an indirect object (io) in Italian, and the equivalent of a direct object (do) in English is a subject (s) in Italian. This is the case of the English verb *to like* (**piacere**, literally *to be pleasing*).

*Carlo **likes** the car.*
S V DO
↓ ↓ ↓
IO V S

A Carlo **piace** la macchina.
to Carlo is pleasing the car

Let us go over this type of transformation step by step:

1. Transformation — Transform the English sentence by turning the subject (s) into an indirect object (io) and the direct object (do) into the subject (s).

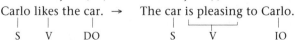

Carlo likes the car. → The car is pleasing to Carlo.
S V DO → S V IO

2. PLACEMENT — Place the indirect object at the beginning
of the sentence.

"to Carlo is pleasing the car"

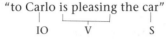

      IO   V   S

You can now express that structure in Italian.

"to Carlo is pleasing the car"
A Carlo piace la macchina.

      IO   V   S

Here is a list of the common verbs which require an indirect object in Italian where English uses a subject.

to regret	dispiacere
to need	occorrere
to be lacking	mancare

Since Italian and English patterns do not coincide in many
cases, it is important to identify the object function within
the language in which you are working.

SUMMARY

The different types of objects in a sentence can be identified
by looking to see if they are introduced by a preposition and,
if so, by which one.

DIRECT OBJECT — An object that receives the action of the verb
directly, without a preposition.

INDIRECT OBJECT — An object that receives the action of the
verb indirectly, through the preposition *to* or *for*.

OBJECT OF A PREPOSITION — An object that receives the action of
the verb through a preposition other than *to* or *for*.

Your ability to recognize the three kinds of objects is essen-
tial. With pronouns, for instance, a different Italian pronoun
is used for the English pronoun *him* depending on whether
him is a direct object (**lo**), an indirect object (**gli**) or an object
of a preposition (**lui**).

WHAT IS AN OBJECT PRONOUN?

An **OBJECT PRONOUN** is a pronoun used as an object of a verb   1
or of a preposition.

> Mary saw *me* at school.

IN ENGLISH

Pronouns change according to their function in the sentence. Pronouns used as subjects are studied in *What is a Subject Pronoun?*, p. 31. We use subject pronouns when we conjugate verbs (see *What is a Verb Conjugation?*, p. 35). Object pronouns are used when a pronoun is either a direct object, indirect object, or object of a preposition   10
(see *What is an Object?*, p. 117).

Except for the pronouns *you* and *it*, the form of the object pronoun is different from the form of the subject pronoun, but the same pronoun form is used as a direct object, indirect object, or object of a preposition.

		SUBJECT PRONOUNS	OBJECT PRONOUNS
SINGULAR			
1st person		I	me
2nd person		you	you
3rd person	{	he	him
		she	her
		it	it
PLURAL			
1st person		we	us
2nd person		you	you
3rd person		they	them

Here are a few examples. As you can see, the object pronoun is always placed after the verb or after the preposition.

> She saw *me*.   30
> direct object → object pronoun

> I lent *him* my car.
> indirect object → object pronoun

> They went out with *her*.
> object of a preposition → object pronoun

IN ITALIAN

Unlike English a different object pronoun is normally used for each kind of object: direct, indirect, and object of a preposition. You will, therefore, have to establish the function of a pronoun so that you can choose the correct Italian form.

DIRECT OBJECT PRONOUNS

First, you have to establish that the Italian verb takes a direct object. Remember that English and Italian verbs don't always take the same type of objects and that when working in Italian you will have to establish the type of object taken by the Italian verb (see pp. 120-2).

Let us look at the Italian direct object pronouns.

DIRECT OBJECT PRONOUNS			
SINGULAR			
1st person		mi	*me*
2nd person		ti	*you* [familiar]
3rd person	masc.	lo	*him, it*
	fem.	la	*her, it*
	masc./fem.	La	*you* [formal]
PLURAL			
1st person		ci	*us*
2nd person		vi	*you* [familiar]
3rd person	masc.	li	*them*
	fem.	le	*them*
	masc.	Li	*you* [formal]
	fem.	Le	*you* [formal]

Direct object pronouns are used as they are in English, but normally they precede the conjugated verb. Consult your textbook for rules about placement.

To see how direct object pronouns are selected, we have divided them into two categories: those which have a one-on-one Italian equivalent and those which require analysis.

"Me, him, her, us"

These direct object pronouns have a one-on-one Italian equivalent. Select the form you need and place it before the conjugated verb: *me* → **mi**, *him* → **lo**, *her* → **la**, *us* → **ci**.

*John sees **me**.*
Giovanni **mi** vede.
*John sees **him**.*
Giovanni **lo** vede.

"You" — There are various equivalents of the direct object pronoun *you* depending on the person or persons being addressed. Follow these steps to select the proper form. 80

1. FORM — Is the familiar or formal form of *you* appropriate?

If familiar:

2. NUMBER — Are you addressing one or more persons?
   ■ one person → singular → **ti**
   ■ more than one person → plural → **vi**

If formal:

2. NUMBER — Are you addressing one or more persons?
   ■ one person → singular → **La** 90
   ■ if more than one person → plural: What is their gender?

3. GENDER — Are you addressing men or women?
   ■ a group of men or men and women → masculine → **Li**
   ■ a group of women → feminine → **Le**

Here are a few examples.

> *Maria, John sees you often.* [you = Maria]
>   1. *Maria* implies familiarity → familiar
>   2. *Maria* is one person → singular
> Maria, Giovanni **ti** vede spesso.

> *Boys, John sees you often.* [you = boys]
>   1. *Boys* implies familiarity → familiar
>   2. *Boys* is more than one person → plural
> Ragazzi, Giovanni **vi** vede spesso. 100

> *Sir, John sees you often.* [you = Sir]
>   1. *Sir* implies formality → formal
>   2. *Sir* is one person → singular
> Signore, Giovanni **La** vede spesso.

> *Mrs. Rossi, John sees you often.* [you = Mrs. Rossi]
>   1. *Mrs. Rossi* implies formality → formal
>   2. *Mrs. Rossi* is one person → singular
> Signora Rossi, Giovanni **La** vede spesso. 110

> *Gentlemen, John sees you often.* [you = Gentlemen]
>   1. *Gentlemen* implies formality → formal
>   2. *Gentlemen* is more than one person → plural
>   3. *Gentlemen* → masculine
> Signori, Giovanni **Li** vede spesso.

> *Young ladies, John sees you often.* [you = young ladies]
>   1. *Young ladies* implies formality → formal
>   2. *Young ladies* is more than one person → plural
>   3. *Young ladies* → feminine
> Signorine, Giovanni **Le** vede spesso.

"It" — The form depends on the gender of its antecedent, i.e., the noun *it* refers to: masculine antecedent → **lo**; feminine antecedent → **la**.

> *Do you see the plane? Yes, I see **it**.*
> 1. ANTECEDENT: *plane* → **l'aero**
> 2. GENDER OF ANTECEDENT: masculine
> 3. SELECTION: **lo**

Vedi l'aero? Si, **lo** vedo.

> *Do you see the car? Yes, I see **it**.*
> 1. ANTECEDENT: *car* → **la macchina**
> 2. GENDER OF ANTECEDENT: feminine
> 3. SELECTION: **la**

Vedi la macchina? Si, **la** vedo.

"Them" — The form depends on the gender of its antecedent, i.e. the noun *them* refers to: masculine antecedent → **li**; feminine antecedent → **le**.

> *Do you see the boys? Yes, I see **them**.*
> 1. ANTECEDENT: *boys* → **i ragazzi**
> 2. GENDER OF ANTECEDENT: masculine
> 3. SELECTION: **li**

Vedi i ragazzi? Si, **li** vedo.

> *Do you see the cars? Yes, I see **them**.*
> 1. ANTECEDENT: *cars* → **le macchine**
> 2. GENDER OF ANTECEDENT: feminine
> 3. SELECTION: **le**

Vedi le macchine? Si, **le** vedo.

INDIRECT OBJECT PRONOUNS

First, you have to establish that the Italian verb takes an indirect object. Remember that English and Italian verbs don't always take the same type of objects and that when working in Italian you will have to establish the type of object taken by the Italian verb (see pp. 120-2).

Let us look at the Italian indirect object pronouns.

INDIRECT OBJECT PRONOUNS		
SINGULAR		
1st person	mi	*to me*
2nd person	ti	*to you* [familiar]
3rd person — masc.	gli	*to him*
3rd person — fem.	le	*to her*
3rd person — masc./fem.	Le	*to you* [formal]
PLURAL		
1st person	ci	*to us*
2nd person	vi	*to you* [familiar]
3rd person	loro	*to them*
3rd person	Loro	*to you* [formal]

To see how indirect object pronouns are selected, we have divided them into two categories: the ones that have a one-on-one Italian equivalent and those which require analysis.

"Me, him, her, us, them"
These indirect object pronouns have a one-on-one Italian equivalent. Select the form you need and place it before the conjugated verb: *to me* → **mi**, *to him* → **gli**, *to her* → **le**, *to us* → **ci**, *to them* → **loro**.

Notice that the *to* preceding the English indirect object pronoun is not expressed in Italian. Except for **loro** and **Loro** which are placed after the verb, the indirect object pronouns normally precede the conjugated verb. Consult your textbook for further rules.

Here are a few examples.

> *John gives the book to me.*
> *John gives me the book.*
>> 1. IDENTIFY THE VERB: to give
>> 2. SELECT THE ITALIAN EQUIVALENT: **dare**
>> 3. IDENTIFY THE PRONOUN OBJECT: me
>>> QUESTION: John gives the book to whom? ANSWER: To me.
>>> *Me* is an indirect object pronoun.
>> 4. SELECT THE ITALIAN EQUIVALENT: **mi**

Giovanni **mi** da il libro.

> *John gives the book to him.*
> *John gives him the book.*

Giovanni **gli** da il libro.

> *John gives the book to them.*
> *John gives them the book.*

Giovanni da **loro** il libro.

placed after the verb

"You" — There are various equivalents of the indirect object pronoun *you* depending on the person or persons being addressed. Follow these steps to select the proper form.

1. FORM — Is the familiar or formal form of *you* appropriate?
If familiar:
2. NUMBER — Are you addressing one or more persons?
 - one person → singular → **ti**
 - more than one person → plural → **vi**
If formal:
2. NUMBER — Are you addressing one or more persons?
 - one person → singular → **Le**
 - if more than one person → plural → **Loro**

170

180

190

200

Here are a few examples.

Girls,
John is giving the book to you. [you = Girls]
John is giving you the book.
Ragazze, Giovanni **vi** da il libro.

Sir (Madam),
John is giving the book to you. [you = Sir/Madam]
John is giving you the book.
Signore (Signora), Giovanni **Le** da il libro.

Gentlemen (Young ladies),
John is giving the book to you. [you = Gentlemen/Young ladies]
John is giving you the book.
Signori (Signorine), Giovanni da **Loro** il libro.

placed after the verb

OBJECT OF PREPOSITION PRONOUNS

First, you have to establish that the Italian verb is followed by a preposition. Remember that English and Italian verbs don't always take the same type of objects and that when working in Italian you will have to establish the type of object taken by the Italian verb (see pp. 120-2).

Let us look at the Italian object of preposition pronouns. (Note that, except for **me** and **te**, the forms are the same as the subject pronouns.)

OBJECT OF PREPOSITION PRONOUNS			
SINGULAR			
1st person		prep. + me	*prep. + me*
2nd person		prep. + te	*prep. + you* [familiar]
	masc.	prep. + lui	*prep. + him*
3rd person	fem.	prep. + lei	*prep. + her*
	masc./fem.	prep. + Lei	*prep. + you* [formal]
PLURAL			
1st person		prep. + noi	*prep. + us*
2nd person		prep. + voi	*prep. + you* [familiar]
3rd person		prep. + loro	*prep. + them*
		prep. + Loro	*prep. + you* [formal]

To see how pronoun objects of a preposition are selected, we have divided them into two categories: the ones that have a one-on-one Italian equivalent and those which require analysis.

"Me, him, her, us, them"

These object of preposition pronouns are merely a question of memorization. Select the form you need and place it after the verb preceded by the appropriate preposition : *me* → **me**, *him* → **lui**, *her* → **lei**, *us* → **noi**, *them* → **loro**.

Here are a few examples.

> *Are they talking about Luigi? No, they are talking **about me**.*
> 1. IDENTIFY THE PREPOSITION: about → **di**
> 2. IDENTIFY THE OBJECT OF THE PREPOSITION: me
> 3. SELECTION: **me**

Parlano di Luigi? No, parlano **di me**.

> *Are you going to the party with Mary? Yes, I'm going **with her**.*

Vai alla festa con Maria? Si, vado **con lei**.

> *Did you receive a letter from your friends?*
> *Yes, I received a letter **from them** yesterday.*

Hai ricevuto una lettera dai tuoi aimici?
Si, ho ricevuto una lettera **da loro** ieri.

"You"—There are various equivalents of the object of preposition pronoun *you* depending on the person or persons being addressed. Follow these steps to select the proper form.

1. FORM — Is the familiar or formal form of *you* appropriate?

If familiar:

2. NUMBER — Are you addressing one or more persons?
   - one person → singular → **te**
   - more than one person → plural → **voi**

If formal:

2. NUMBER — Are you addressing one or more persons?
   - one person → singular → **Lei**
   - if more than one person → plural → **Loro**

Here are some examples.

> *Carla, I would like to speak **with you**.*

Carla, vorrei parlare **con te**.

> *Boys, I would like to speak **with you**.*

Ragazzi, vorrei parlare **con voi**.

> *Miss, I would like to speak **with you**.*

Signorina, vorrei parlare **con Lei**.

> *Gentlemen, I would like to speak **with you**.*

Signori, vorrei parlare **con Loro**.

In Italian a noun referring to a thing is not generally replaced by a pronoun when it follows a preposition. For example, in answer to the question "Is the book on the table?" one does not say "Yes, the book is *on it.*" Rather, one repeats the noun: "Yes, the book is *on the table.*" Similarly, in answer to the question "Do you live near the mountains?" one does not usually say, "Yes, I live *near them.*" Instead, one repeats the noun: "Yes, I live *near the mountains.*"

CAREFUL — Remember that English and Italian verbs don't always take the same type of objects and that when working in Italian you will have to establish the type of object taken by the Italian verb (see pp. 120-2).

STRESSED AND UNSTRESSED PRONOUNS

The direct and indirect object pronouns already treated in this chapter are called CONJUNCTIVE or UNSTRESSED PRONOUNS and they usually precede the verb.

The object of preposition forms of the pronoun are also used for emphasis or contrast in place of the direct or indirect object pronouns. In this function, they are called DISJUNCTIVE or STRESSED PRONOUNS and they are placed after the verb.

*I see **her**.* [unstressed]
La vedo.
|
unstressed pronoun
direct object
precedes the verb **vedo**

*I see **her**.* [stressed: "I see *her* and no one else."]
Vedo **lei**.
|
stressed pronoun
direct object
follows the verb **vedo**

*I gave the book **to her**.* [unstressed]
Le ho dato il libro.
|
unstressed pronoun
indirect object
precedes the verb **ho dato**

*I gave the book **to her**.* [stressed: "...*to her* and to no one else."]
Ho dato il libro **a lei**.
|
stressed pronoun
indirect object
follows the verb **ho dato**

SUMMARY

330

Here is a chart of subject and object pronouns that you can use as reference :

		UNSTRESSED		STRESSED &
		DIRECT	INDIRECT	OBJECT OF
	SUBJECT	OBJECT	OBJECT	PREPOSITION
SINGULAR				
1st person	io	mi	mi	me
2nd person	tu	ti	ti	te
3rd person {	lui masc.	lo	gli	lui
	lei fem.	la	le	lei
	Lei	La	Le	Lei
PLURAL				
1st person	noi	ci	ci	noi
2nd person	voi	vi	vi	voi
3rd person {	loro {	li masc.⎫ le fem.⎬	loro	loro
	Loro {	Li masc.⎫ Le fem.⎬	Loro	Loro

340

Object pronouns are challenging and you will need to consult your textbook for additional rules.

350

WHAT IS AN INTERROGATIVE PRONOUN?

1 An INTERROGATIVE PRONOUN is a word that replaces a noun and introduces a question.

> *Who* lives here? My friend lives here.

IN ENGLISH
Different interrogative pronouns are used depending on whether you are referring to a "person" (this category includes human beings and live animals) or a "thing" (this category includes objects and ideas). Also, the interrogative pronoun referring to persons changes according to its function in the sentence.

10 **IN ITALIAN**
As in English, a different interrogative pronoun is used depending on whether the pronoun replaces a person or a thing. Also, as in English, an interrogative pronoun can be a subject, a direct object, an indirect object, or an object of a preposition.

"WHO, WHOM"
IN ENGLISH
Who is used for the subject of the sentence.

20 > *Who* lives here?
> |
> subject

Whom is used for the direct object, indirect object, and the object of a preposition.

> *Whom* do you know here?
> |
> direct object

> To *whom* did you speak?
> |
> indirect object

30 > From *whom* did you get the book?
> |
> object of preposition *from*

In colloquial English, *who* is often used instead of *whom*, and prepositions are placed at the end of the sentence, separated from the interrogative pronoun to which they are linked (see dangling prepositions, pp. 112-3).

> *Who* do you know here?
> |
> instead of *whom*

Who did you speak to?

instead of *whom*   preposition

Who did you get the book from?

instead of *whom*   preposition

IN ITALIAN

Who or *whom* → **chi**

> **Chi** vive qui?
> *Who lives here?*
>
> **Chi** conosci qui?
> *Whom do you know here?*

When the interrogative pronoun is used as an indirect object it is preceded by the preposition **a**. It will therefore be necessary to restructure the sentence.

> *Who are you speaking to?* → *To whom are you speaking?*
>
> subject form of   preposition   object form of interrogative
> interrogative
> **A chi** parli?

When the interrogative pronoun is used as an object of a preposition it is preceded by a preposition. It will therefore be necessary to restructure the sentence.

> *Who did you get the book from?* → *From whom did you get the book?*
> **Da chi** hai avuto il libro?

"WHOSE"
IN ENGLISH

Whose is the possessive form and is used to ask about possession or ownership.

> *Whose* pencil is this?
>
> possessive

> They are nice cars. *Whose* are they?
>
> possessive

IN ITALIAN

Whose → **di chi**. To use the correct word order in Italian, restructure the question by replacing *whose* with *of whom* and invert the word order of the subject and verb.

> *Whose car is it?*
> **Di chi** è la macchina?
> [word-for-word: *of whom is the car*]
>
> *Whose keys are they?*
> **Di chi** sono le chiavi?
> [word-for-word: *of whom are the keys*]

"WHAT"
IN ENGLISH

What refers only to things, and the same form is used for subject, direct object, indirect object, and the object of a preposition.

> *What* happened?
> |
> subject

> *What* do you want?
> |
> direct object

> *What* do you cook with?
> |
> object of preposition *with*

IN ITALIAN

What → **che** or **che cosa**, or just **cosa**. They are interchangeable and invariable. The same form is used for subject, direct object, indirect object, and the object of a preposition.

> ***What*** *happened?*
> **Che** è successo?

> ***What*** *do you want?*
> **Che** vuoi?

> ***What*** *do you cook* ***with?*** →
> ***With what*** *do you cook?*
> **Con che** cucini?

"WHICH ONE, WHICH ONES"
IN ENGLISH

Which one, which ones can refer to both persons and things; they are used in questions that request the selection of one (*which one*, singular) or several (*which ones*, plural) from a group. The words *one* and *ones* are often omitted. These interrogative pronouns may be used as a subject, direct object, indirect object, and object of a preposition.

> There are two teachers here. *Which one* teaches Italian?
> |
> singular subject

> I have two cars. *Which one* do you want to take?
> |
> singular direct object

> There are many children here. *Which ones* do you want to play *with?* →
> **Restructured:** with *which ones* do you want to play?
> |
> plural object of the preposition *with*

IN ITALIAN

Which one, which ones → **quale, quali**. There are two forms to agree in number with the noun replaced, *which one* (singular) or *which ones* (plural). If the English word *one* or *ones* is not expressed, look at the verb to establish number: if the verb is singular → **quale**; if the verb is plural → **quali**.

130

> *There are two teachers here. **Which one** teaches Italian?*
> Ci sono due insegnanti qui. **Quale** insegna italiano?
>
> *I have two cars. **Which one** do you want to take?*
> Ho due macchine. **Quale** vuoi prendere?
>
> *There are many children. With **which ones** do you want to play?*
> Ci sono molti bambini. Con **quali** vuoi giocare?

"WHAT IS...? WHAT ARE...?"

Questions beginning with *what is...?* or *what are...?* can be translated into Italian by either **che + essere...?** or **quale/quali) + essere...?**, depending on what the expected answer will be.

140

- when the expected answer is a definition → **che + essere...?**

> ***What is** poetry?*
> The expected answer is a definition of poetry.
> **Che è** la poesia?

- when the expected answer is one of a number of choices and answers the question *which one(ones)* of many → **quale/quali) + essere...?**

150

> ***What is** your favorite novel?*
> The expected answer will explain which novel of the many that exist is your favorite.
> **Quale è** il tuo romanzo preferito?

There is another interrogative pronoun that we will now examine separately since it does not follow the same pattern as above.

"HOW MUCH, HOW MANY"

IN ENGLISH

These interrogative pronouns are a rare example of pronouns that change form to agree in number with the noun they replace: *how much* (singular), *how many* (plural).

160

> I have some money. *How much* do you need?
>
> singular pronoun
>
> I have some stamps. *How many* do you need?
>
> plural pronoun

IN ITALIAN

This interrogative pronoun has four forms that change according to the gender and number of the antecedent, that is, the noun replaced by the pronoun: singular → **quanto (-a)**; plural → **quanti (-e)**.

Let us look at a two examples.

I have some money today. ***How much*** *do you want?*

1. IDENTIFY ANTECEDENT: *money* → **denaro**
2. GENDER & NUMBER OF ANTECEDENT: masculine singular
3. SELECTION: **quanto**

Ho del denaro oggi. **Quanto** vuoi?

There were ten students present. ***How many*** *voted in favor?*

1. IDENTIFY ANTECEDENT: *students* → **studenti**
2. GENDER & NUMBER OF ANTECEDENT: masculine plural
3. SELECTION: **quanti**

C'erano dieci studenti presenti. **Quanti** hanno votato a favore?

WHAT IS A DEMONSTRATIVE PRONOUN?

A **DEMONSTRATIVE PRONOUN** is a word that replaces a noun pre- viously mentioned, the **ANTECEDENT**, as if pointing to it. Demonstrative comes from *demonstrate,* to show.

> Which book are you buying? *This one.*
> |
> antecedent

IN ENGLISH

English demonstrative pronouns change form according to the number of the noun they replace and according to the relationship of that noun with the speaker.

As with the demonstrative adjectives, *this (one), these* refer to persons or objects near the speaker; *that (one), those* to persons or objects away from the speaker.

> Here are two suitcases. *This one* is big and *that one* is small.
> The books are on the shelves. *These* are in Italian, *those* in English.

IN ITALIAN

Demonstrative pronouns are related to the demonstrative adjectives (see *What is a Demonstrative Adjective?,* p. 107): forms of **questo** or **quello.**

To POINT OUT ▼	SINGULAR		PLURAL	
	masc.	fem.	masc.	fem.
items near the speaker *this (one), these*	questo	questa	questi	queste
items away from the speaker *that (one), those*	quello	quella	quelli	quelle

As pronouns, these words replace the demonstrative adjec- tive + noun; they will agree in number and gender with the noun replaced.

To choose the correct form, follow these steps.

1. ANTECEDENT — Determine the antecedent.
2. GENDER & NUMBER — Determine the gender and number of the antecedent.
3. SELECTION — Based on Steps 1 and 2 choose the cor- rect form from the chart.

Let us apply these steps to some examples.

Which book do you want? ***This one.***
1. ANTECEDENT: *book* → **libro**
2. GENDER & NUMBER OF ANTECEDENT: masculine singular
3. SELECTION: **questo**

Quale libro vuoi? **Questo.**

Which houses did you build? ***These.***
1. ANTECEDENT: *houses* → **case**
2. GENDER & NUMBER OF ANTECEDENT: feminine plural
3. SELECTION: **queste**

Quali case hai costruito? **Queste.**

Which book do you want? ***That one.***
1. ANTECEDENT: *book* → **libro**
2. GENDER & NUMBER OF ANTECEDENT: masculine singular
3. SELECTION: **quello**

Quale libro vuoi? **Quello.**

Which houses did you build? ***Those.***
1. ANTECEDENT: *houses* → **case**
2. GENDER & NUMBER OF ANTECEDENT: feminine plural
3. SELECTION: **quelle**

Quali case hai costruito? **Quelle.**

There is another demonstrative pronoun which we will now examine separately because it does not follow the same pattern as above.

"THE ONE, THE ONES"

IN ENGLISH

The demonstrative pronouns *the one* and *the ones,* unlike *this one* and *that one,* do not point out a specific object, but instead introduce a clause (see p. 81 and p. 142) that gives us additional information about an object and helps us identify it. There is a singular form *the one* and a plural form *the ones.* They are often followed by the relative pronoun *that* or *which* (see *What is a Relative Pronoun?,* p. 142).

> Which house did you buy? *The one* over there.
> CLAUSE: "the one over there" gives us additional information about the house.
> NUMBER: *The one* is singular.

> What books do you want? *The ones (that)* I gave you.
> CLAUSE: "the ones that I gave you" gives us additional information about the books. Notice that the relative pronoun *that* can be omitted.
> NUMBER: *The ones* is plural.

IN ITALIAN

The equivalent of the English pronouns *the one, the ones* is a form of the Italian demonstrative pronoun **quello**. It can be used in two ways: 1. to introduce a clause and 2. to show possession.

In both cases, follow these steps to choose the correct form of **quello.**

1. ANTECEDENT — Find the antecedent.
2. GENDER & NUMBER — Determine the gender and number of the antecedent.
3. SELECTION — Based on steps 1 and 2, choose the appropriate form.

■ to introduce a clause

> *Which house did you buy? **The one** over there.*
>   1. ANTECEDENT: *house* → **casa**
>   2. GENDER & NUMBER OF ANTECEDENT: feminine singular
>   3. SELECTION: **quella**
> Quale casa hai comprato? **Quella** là.

> *Which books do you want? **The ones** I gave you.*
>   1. ANTECEDENT: *books* → **libri**
>   2. GENDER & NUMBER OF ANTECEDENT: masculine plural
>   3. SELECTION: **quelli**
> Quali libri vuoi? **Quelli** che ti ho dato.

■ to show possession

Because the possessive cannot be expressed in Italian with the English apostrophe structure (see *What is the Possessive?*, p. 20), an alternative structure is used which is equivalent to *the one of.*

Just as "my father's house" can only be expressed in Italian by a structure which is word-for-word "the house of my father," the phrase "my father's" is expressed by a structure which is word-for-word *"the one of* my father." In this case also **quello** agrees in gender and number with its antecedent.

Let us apply the rules to the following examples.

> *Which house are you selling? **My father's.***
> My father's → *the one* of my father
>   1. ANTECEDENT: *house* → **casa**
>   2. GENDER & NUMBER OF ANTECEDENT: feminine singular.
>   3. SELECTION: **quella**
> Quale casa vendi? **Quella di mio padre.**

> *Which books are you reading? **The teacher's.***
> The teacher's → *the ones* of the teacher
>   1. ANTECEDENT: *books* → **libri**
>   2. GENDER & NUMBER OF ANTECEDENT: masculine plural.
>   3. SELECTION: **quelli**
> Quali libri leggi? **Quelli del professore.**

90

100

110

120

CHAPTER

44

WHAT IS A POSSESSIVE PRONOUN?

A **POSSESSIVE PRONOUN** is a word that replaces a noun and indicates the possessor of that noun. Possessive comes from *possess,* to own.

> Whose house is that? It's *mine.*

IN ENGLISH

Here is a list of the possessive pronouns.

SINGULAR

1st person		mine
2nd person		yours
3rd person	masc.	his
	fem.	hers
	neuter	its

PLURAL

1st person	ours
2nd person	yours
3rd person	theirs

Possessive pronouns never change their form, regardless of the thing possessed; they refer only to the possessor.

> Is that your house? Yes, it's *mine.*
> Are those your keys? Yes, they're *mine.*
>> The same possessive pronoun, *mine,* is used, although the objects possessed are different in number *(house* is singular, *keys* is plural).

> John's car is blue. *His* is blue.
> Mary's car is blue. *Hers* is blue.
>> Although the object possessed is the same, *car,* the possessive pronoun is different because the possessor is different *(John* is masculine singular; *Mary* is feminine singular).

IN ITALIAN

The possessive pronoun refers to the possessor, but, like all Italian pronouns, it must agree in gender and number with its antecedent. Therefore, there are masculine and feminine forms in both the singular and plural. The forms of the possessive pronouns are identical to the forms of the possessive adjective, and they are also preceded by the definite article. The only difference between the possessive adjectives and the possessive pronouns is that the possessive adjective is followed by the noun it modifies, whereas the possessive pronoun replaces the noun.

Io leggo le mie riviste; tu leggi **le tue**.

antecedent → fem. pl.   fem. pl.

    Le tue refers to the possessor, **tu** *you,* but agrees in gender and
number with the noun being replaced, **rivisite** *magazines.*

I am reading my magazines; you are reading ***yours***.

Noi vediamo spesso le nostre sorelle; voi non vedete **le vostre**.

        antecedent → fem. pl.   fem. pl.

    Le vostre refers to the possessor, **voi** *you,* but agrees in
gender and number with the noun being replaced, **sorelle**
sisters.

We see our sisters often; you don't see ***yours***.

For the different forms, use the chart on p. 104 as reference.

WHAT IS A RELATIVE PRONOUN?

A **RELATIVE PRONOUN** is a word that serves two purposes:

1. As a pronoun it usually stands for a noun or another pronoun previously mentioned. The noun or pronoun referred to is called **THE ANTECEDENT**.

This is the boy *who* broke the window.
|
antecedent

The antecedent is part of the **MAIN CLAUSE**, that is, a group of words containing a subject and a verb expressing a complete thought. A main clause can stand alone as a complete sentence.

2. It introduces a **SUBORDINATE CLAUSE**, that is, a group of words having a subject and verb, but not expressing a complete thought.

main clause   subordinate clause

This is the boy *who* broke the window.
           | |
         subject verb

["who broke the window" is not a complete sentence]

The above subordinate clause is also called a **RELATIVE CLAUSE** because it is introduced by the relative pronoun *who*. The relative clause gives us additional information about the antecedent *boy*.

There are also relative pronouns which are used without an expressed antecedent (see pp. 149-50).

CONSTRUCTION OF RELATIVE CLAUSES
IN ENGLISH

Relative clauses are very common. We use them every day without giving much thought as to why and how we construct them. The relative pronoun allows us to combine in a single sentence two thoughts which have a common element.

SENTENCE A   The students passed the exam.

SENTENCE B   The students attended class regularly.

The common element to both sentences is the noun *students*. *Students* in sentence A, the main clause, will be the antecedent. *Students* in sentence B, the subordinate clause, will be replaced by the relative pronoun *who* or t*hat*.

relative clause

The students *who* attended class regularly passed the exam.

antecedent relative pronoun

SENTENCE A   The man was young.
SENTENCE B   We were talking about the man.

The common element to both sentences is the noun *man*. *Man* in sentence A, the main clause, will be the antecedent. *Man* in sentence B, the subordinate clause, will be replaced by the relative pronoun *who(m)* or *that*.

There are three possible ways to combine these two sentences.

1. The man *that* we were talking about was young.

antecedent   relative clause

The relative clause "that we were talking *about*" has a dangling preposition (see p. 112).

2. The man we were talking about was young.

antecedent   relative clause

The relative pronoun beginning the relative clause *"who(m) or that* we were talking about" can be omitted.

3. The man *about whom* we were talking was young.

antecedent   relative clause

To avoid the dangling preposition, the preposition *about* can be placed at the beginning of the relative clause.

The fact that the relative pronoun can be omitted makes it sometimes difficult to identify relative clauses in English.

IN ITALIAN

As in English, two separate sentences can be combined with a relative pronoun. However, be sure to remember the following two differences:

1. the relative pronoun can never be omitted as in example 2 above.
2. a preposition cannot be dangling at the end of the relative clause as in 1 above. It must be placed at the beginning of the clause followed by its object, the relative pronoun as in example 3 above.

SELECTION OF RELATIVE PRONOUNS

A relative pronoun can have different functions in the relative clause. It can be subject, direct object, indirect object, or object of a preposition. Since your selection of the relative pronoun will usually depend on its function, we shall study each function separately.

IN ENGLISH

In many cases the selection of a relative pronoun depends not only on its function in the relative clause, but also on whether the antecedent is a "person" (this category includes human beings and live animals) or a "thing" (this category includes objects and ideas).

IN ITALIAN

The main difference between the use of relative pronouns in Italian and English is that, unlike English, where the relative pronoun can sometimes be omitted (see example 2, p. 143), the relative pronoun must always be expressed. Also, a relative pronoun is not affected by whether its antecedent is a person or a thing.

SUBJECT OF THE RELATIVE CLAUSE
IN ENGLISH

There are three relative pronouns that can be used as subjects of a relative clause, depending on whether the relative pronoun refers to a person or to a thing.

Person

Who or *that* is used for the subject of the clause.

> She is the only student *who* answers all the time.
> She is the only student *that* answers all the time.
> |
>   antecedent
> *Who* is the subject of *answers*. *That* is the subject of *answers*.

Thing

Which or *that* is used for the subject of the clause.

> This is the book *which* is so popular.
> This is the movie *that* is so popular.
> |
>   antecedent
> *Which* is the subject of *is*. *That* is the subject of *is*.

IN ITALIAN

There is only one relative pronoun that can be used as subject of a relative clause → **che.**

> È la sola studentessa **che** risponde sempre.
> *She is the only student **who** answers all the time.*
> *She is the only student **that** answers all the time.*

> Questo è il libro **che** è così popolare.
> *This is the book **which** is so popular.*
> *This is the book **that** is so popular.*

DIRECT OBJECT OF THE RELATIVE CLAUSE
IN ENGLISH

There are three relative pronouns that can be used as direct objects of a relative clause, depending on whether the relative pronoun refers to a person or a thing. We have indicated relative pronouns in parentheses because they are often omitted.

Person

Whom or *that* is used as a direct object of a clause.

130

> This is the student *(whom)* I saw yesterday.
> This is the student *(that)* I saw yesterday.
> |
> antecedent

> *Whom* is the direct object of *saw*. *That* is the direct object of *saw*. *(I* is the subject of the relative clause.)

Thing

Which or *that* is used as a direct object of a clause.

> This is the book *(which)* Paul bought.
> This is the book *(that)* Paul bought.
> |
> antecedent

140

> *Which* is the direct object of *bought*. *That* is the direct object of *bought*. *(Paul* is the subject of the relative clause.)

IN ITALIAN

There is only one relative pronoun that can be used as direct object of a relative clause → **che.**

> Questo è lo studente **che** ho visto ieri.
> *This is the student* **(that/whom)** *I saw yesterday.*

> Ecco il libro **che** ho comprato.
> *Here is the book* **(which/that)** *I bought.*

150

INDIRECT OBJECT OR OBJECT OF A PREPOSITION IN THE RELATIVE CLAUSE

The relative pronoun as an indirect object and as an object of a preposition involve prepositions. As an indirect object it is the object of the preposition *to* or *for* and as an object of a preposition it is the object of any preposition other than *to* or *for* (see pp. 118-9).

It is difficult to identify the function of a relative pronoun as an indirect object or an object of a preposition because in English the preposition is often placed at the end of the sentence, separated from the relative pronoun to which it is linked. This separation of a preposition from its object is called a DANGLING PREPOSITION (see p. 112).

160

To make it easier for you to identify a relative pronoun as an indirect object or an object of a preposition, you will have to restructure the sentence as follows:

1. place the preposition right after the antecedent
2. reinstate the relative pronoun after the preposition

See the examples under "In English" below.

IN ENGLISH

There are two relative pronouns used as indirect objects and objects of a preposition, depending on whether you are referring to a person or a thing.

Person

Whom is used as an indirect object or as an object of a preposition.

Here is the student I was speaking to.
　　　　　　antecedent　　　dangling preposition

Spoken English	→	Restructured
Here is the student		Here is the student
I was speaking *to.*		*to whom* I was speaking.

relative clause

Here is the student *to whom* I was speaking.
　　　　　　　relative pronoun
　　　　　　　indirect object

Here is the student I was talking about.
　　　　　　antecedent　　　dangling preposition

Spoken English	→	Restructured
Here is the student		Here is the student
I was speaking *about.*		*about whom* I was speaking.

relative clause

Here is the student *about whom* I was speaking.
　　　　antecedent　　relative pronoun
　　　　　　　object of preposition

Thing

Which is used as an indirect object or as an object of a preposition.

Here is the museum he gave the painting to.
　　　　　antecedent　　　　　dangling preposition

Spoken English	→	Restructured
Here is the museum		Here is the museum
he gave the painting *to.*		*to which* he gave the painting.

relative clause

Here is the museum *to which* he gave the painting.

antecedent   relative pronoun
indirect object

This is the book I was speaking about.

antecedent   dangling preposition

Spoken English	→	**Restructured**
Here is the book		Here is the book
I was speaking *about.*		*about which* I was speaking.

relative clause

This is the book *about which* I was speaking.

antecedent   relative pronoun
object of preposition

IN ITALIAN

There is only one relative pronoun that can be used as indirect object or the object of a preposition of a relative clause → **cui**.

*Here is the student I was speaking **to**.*
Restructured → *Here is the student **to whom** I was speaking.*
Ecco lo studente **a cui** parlavo.

*Here is the student I was speaking **about**.*
Restructured → *Here is the student **about whom** I was speaking.*
Ecco lo studente **di cui** parlavo.

*Here is the museum he gave the painting **to**.*
Restructured → *Here is the museum **to which** he gave the painting.*
Ecco il museo **a cui** ha donato il quadro.

*These are the books I was speaking **about**.*
Restructured →*These are the books **about which** I was speaking.*
Questi sono i libri **di cui** parlavo.

POSSESSIVE MODIFIER IN THE RELATIVE CLAUSE
IN ENGLISH

Whose is the only relative pronoun that can be used as a possessive modifier in a relative clause. Its antecedent is usually a person, but it can be a thing.

Here is the woman *whose* pearls were stolen.

antecedent   possessive modifying
person   *pearls*

Look at the house *whose* roof burned.

antecedent   possessive modifying
thing   *roof*

210

220

230

240

IN ITALIAN

There is only one relative pronoun that can be used as a possessive modifier → **cui** preceded by a definite article. The definite article must agree in gender and number with the noun it modifies which immediately follows **cui**.

250

*Here is the woman **whose** pearls were stolen.*
Ecco la donna **le cui** perle sono state rubate.

            fem. pl.   noun modified → fem. pl.

*Look at the house **whose** roof burned.*
Guarda la casa **il cui** tetto è bruciato.

          masc. sing.   noun modified → masc. sing.

SUMMARY

The following chart provides a summary of the relative pronouns.

260

ENGLISH		ITALIAN	
SUBJECT			
person	*who, that*	person	} che
thing	*that, which*	thing	
DIRECT OBJECT			
person	*whom, that*	person	} che
thing	*that, which*	thing	
INDIRECT OBJECT			
person	*to (for) whom*	person	} a cui
thing	*to (for) which*	thing	
OBJECT OF PREPOSITION			
person	*whom*	person	} preposition + cui
thing	*which*	thing	
POSSESSIVE			
	whose		il, la i, le + cui

270

To find the correct relative pronoun you must go through the following steps.

1. RELATIVE CLAUSE — Find the relative clause. Restructure the English clause if there is a dangling preposition.
2. RELATIVE PRONOUN — Find or add the relative pronoun.

280

3. ANTECEDENT — Find the antecedent.
4. FUNCTION OF PRONOUN — Establish the function of the relative pronoun in the Italian clause.

SUBJECT — if the relative pronoun is the subject of the English clause, it will be the subject of the Italian clause → **che**

DIRECT OBJECT — if the Italian verb takes a direct object → **che**

INDIRECT OBJECT — if the Italian verb takes an indirect object → **a cui**

OBJECT OF A PREPOSITION — preposition + **cui**

POSSESSIVE — definite article + **cui** + noun indicating the person or thing possessed. Identify the gender and number of the person or thing possessed in order to select the corresponding article (**il, la i,** or **le**).

5. SELECTION — Based on the above steps, select the Italian form.

Let us apply these steps to some examples.

*The students **who** attended class regularly passed the exam.*
1. RELATIVE CLAUSE: who attended class regularly
2. RELATIVE PRONOUN: who
3. ANTECEDENT: students
4. FUNCTION OF RELATIVE PRONOUN: subject of the relative clause
5. SELECTION: **che**

Gli studenti **che** hanno frequentato regolarmente le lezioni sono stati promossi.

The boys we were talking about were young.
1. RELATIVE CLAUSE: we were talking about
   Restructured→ about *whom* we were talking
2. RELATIVE PRONOUN: whom
3. ANTECEDENT: the boys
4. FUNCTION OF RELATIVE PRONOUN IN ITALIAN: object of preposition *about*
5. SELECTION: **cui**

I ragazzi **di cui** parlavamo erano giovani.

*Dante is a poet **whose** works are well known.*
1. RELATIVE CLAUSE: whose works are well known
2. RELATIVE PRONOUN: whose
3. ANTECEDENT: poet
4. FUNCTION OF RELATIVE PRONOUN IN ITALIAN: possessive
   ITEM POSSESSED: *works* → **le opere**
5. SELECTION: **cui**

Dante è un poeta **le cui** opere sono ben conosciute.

Relative clauses can be difficult to construct and this handbook provides only a simple outline. Refer to your Italian textbook for additional rules.

RELATIVE PRONOUNS WITHOUT ANTECEDENTS

There are relative pronouns that do not refer to a specific noun or pronoun within the same sentence. Instead these relative pronouns refer back to a whole idea or to an antecedent that is not expressed.

IN ENGLISH

There are two relative pronouns that may be used without an antecedent: *what* and *which*.

What — does not refer to a specific noun or pronoun.

I don't know w*h*at happened.
|
no expressed antecedent

Here is w*h*at I read.
|
no expressed antecedent

Which — refers to a clause, not to a specific noun or pronoun.

You speak many languages, whi*c*h is an asset.
|_____| |
clause   refers to an idea contained in the clause

She didn't do well, wh*i*ch is too bad.
|_____| |
clause   refers to an idea contained in the clause

IN ITALIAN

What → **quello che** or **ciò che** — does not refer to a specific noun or pronoun

I don't know **what** *happened.*
Non so **quello che** è successo.
Non so **ciò che** è successo.

Here is **what** *I read.*
Ecco **quello che** ho letto.
Ecco **ciò che** ho letto.

Which → **il che** — refers to a clause, not to a specific noun or pronoun

You speak many languages, **which** *is an asset.*
Parli molte lingue, **il che** è un vantaggio.

Chi is another frequently used relative pronoun without an antecedent. It is the equivalent of the seldom used English expressions *he who, those who,* etc.

Chi *studia, impara.*
He who studies, learns.
Those who study, learn.

WHAT ARE POSITIVE AND NEGATIVE INDEFINITES?

INDEFINITES are words which refer to persons, things or periods of time that are not specific. Indefinite words can be positive or negative (see *What are Affirmative and Negative Sentences?*, p. 42). 1

 I was hoping *someone* would come, but *nobody* came.
    positive indefinite   negative indefinite

IN ENGLISH

Common positive indefinites are often paired with their corresponding negative indefinites that are opposite in meaning. 10

POSITIVE		NEGATIVE
someone, somebody		
anyone, anybody	≠	no one, nobody
everyone, everybody		
something		
anything	≠	nothing
everything		
some		
any	≠	not any, none
every		
some day		
sometimes	≠	never
always		
ever		
somewhere	≠	nowhere
everywhere		

The negative indefinite words enable us to respond negatively to questions which contain a positive indefinite word. 30

QUESTION	Is *anyone* coming tonight?
ANSWER	*No one.*
QUESTION	Do you have *anything* for me?
ANSWER	*Nothing.*
QUESTION	Have you *ever* gone to Europe?
ANSWER	*Never.*

English sentences can be made negative in one of two ways:

1. with the word *not* before the main verb .

I am studying.

I am *not* studying.

2. with a negative word in any part of the sentence

No one is coming.

He has *never* seen a movie.

English does not allow DOUBLE NEGATIVES; i.e., more than one negative word in a sentence. When a sentence contains the negative word *not,* only a positive indefinite can be used in that sentence.

I have *nothing.*

                negative word

I do *not* have *anything.*

     not   positive indefinite word

"I do *not* have *nothing.*" [incorrect English]

     not   negative indefinite word

This sentence contains a double negative: *not* and *nothing.*

IN ITALIAN

As in English, the positive and negative indefinite negative words exist as pairs of opposites.

Positive		Negative	
someone, somebody	qualcuno		
anyone, anybody	qualcuno, chiunque	nessuno	no one, nobody
everyone, everybody	ognuno, tutti		
something	qualcosa	niente, nulla	nothing
anything			
everything	ogni cosa, tutto		
some, any	qualche	nessuno	not any, none
every	ogni, tutti		
some day	un giorno		
sometimes	qualche volta	mai	never, not ever
always	sempre		
ever	mai		
somewhere	(in, da) qualche parte	(in, da) nessuna	nowhere
everywhere	dappertutto	parte	

As in English, the negative indefinites can be used to give negative one-word answers to questions containing positive indefinites.

QUESTION   Ha detto **qualcosa?**   80
                         |
                      positive

ANSWER   **Niente.**
                 |
               negative

*Did he say **anything?***
Nothing.

CAREFUL — Contrary to English, double negatives must be used in Italian when a sentence is made negative by the use of **non** *not* before the verb. A positive indefinite cannot be used in a negative sentence.   90

Non ho niente.
 | |
not   negative indefinite *(nothing)*

*I do **not** have **anything**.*
      | |
    not   positive indefinite

The following formula for the usage of positive and negative indefinites in English and Italian will help you use them correctly.

English   *not* + verb + positive indefinite or indefinites
Italian   **non** + verb + negative indefinite or indefinites

*I do **not** see **anybody**.*   100
      | |
    not + positive indefinite

Non vedo nessuno.
 | |
non + negative indefinite

[word-for-word: *"I do **not** see **nobody**"*]

Follow these steps to find the Italian equivalent of an English sentence with *not* + an indefinite word:

1. INDEFINITE — Locate the indefinite word in the English sentence.
2. NEGATIVE — From the chart choose the negative indefinite that is the opposite of the English positive indefinite.
3. RESTRUCTURE — Restructure the English sentence using *not*   110
   + the negative word chosen under No. 2 above.

Let us apply these three steps to the following sentences.

*I do **not** want to eat **anything**.*
   1. IDENTIFY THE INDEFINITE: anything
   2. SELECT THE NEGATIVE: nothing
   3. RESTRUCTURE: "I do not want to eat *nothing*"
Non voglio mangiare **niente.**

*I **don't** (do **not**) know **anyone** here.*
   1. IDENTIFY THE INDEFINITE: anyone
   2. SELECT THE NEGATIVE: no one   120
   3. RESTRUCTURE: "I don't know *no one* here"
Non conosco nessuno qui.